RAILWAY OPERATION FOR THE MODELLER

Modelling The Steam Era

Bob Essery

MIDLAND

An imprint of
Ian Allan Publishing

CONTENTS

RAILWAY OPERATION FOR THE MODELLER:
Bob Essery © 2003

ISBN 1 85780 168 7

First published in 2003 by Midland Publishing
4 Watling Drive, Hinckley, Leics, LE10 3EY, England.
Tel: 01455 233 747, fax: 01455 233 737
E-mail: midlandbooks@compuserve.com

Design concept and layout
© Midland Publishing and
Stephen Thompson Associates

Midland Publishing is an imprint of
Ian Allan Publishing Ltd.

Printed in England by Ian Allan Printing Ltd
Molesey Road, Hersham, Surrey, KT12 4RG

Title page: **This is a model! 'The West
Riding' express, made up of a mixture of
BR Mk 1, Gresley and Thompson coaches,
hauled by Class A1 Pacific No 60136,**
Alcazar, **passes Stoke Summit signal box.**
Tony Wright

INTRODUCTION

The railway preservation movement does a remarkable job of preserving, restoring and running equipment that mostly stems from the steam age. However, despite their best efforts, the preserved railways cannot provide a complete recreation of the past. For example, today's health and safety regulations forbid many of the working practices that were once part of the traditional steam railway, but most of all, it is the total absence of freight and mineral traffic, once the lifeblood of the system, that makes it impossible for our heritage railways, to truly represent the steam era.

Therefore in order to demonstrate how the Victorian steam railway was operated, we must rely upon models set out to illustrate the period and practices being represented, with their movements replicating, as far as possible, the train workings of yesteryear. If this can be achieved then we can recapture, in model form, many scenes from the railway age that can no longer be seen on full size railways.

It is clear to me that with each passing day, our knowledge and in particular experience, of the steam railway is diminished as those who knew it pass on. Although research can be both interesting and rewarding in itself, it is infinitely more rewarding if it can be put to good use. Therefore, whilst I believe that railway enthusiasts in general will find this book interesting as an introduction to the operating practices of the steam railway, I also hope that modellers will use the book as a guide to enable them to try to make the operating practices on their model railways as accurate as possible.

At this point readers are entitled to ask, 'What qualifications does the author have that enables him to write this book?' A good question that deserves an answer. Perhaps I should at this point present my railway CV. Railways in one form or another have always played an important part in my life. Amongst my earliest memories are those of my father lifting me to his shoulder level so that I could see the trains that were clearly visible across Webb Lane from our front garden in Hall Green, a district in Birmingham. Sadly my father died after spending many months in a sanatorium when I was six years of age, so the influence of railways must date from the early to mid 1930s, when I was five or perhaps even younger. Later, my younger brother and I were allowed by our mother to join other boys who sat on the fence in Webb Lane to watch the trains go by. This marked the beginning of my active interest in railways.

When I was eleven, my family moved to the Small Heath district of Birmingham. This enabled me to spend many hours watching trains from either the bridge to the south of Tyseley station or on the Golden Hillock Road bridge at Small Heath & Sparkbrook station.

Unlike Webb Lane, where the traffic over the North Warwickshire line was not particularly heavy, Small Heath & Sparkbrook was on the line between London and Birmingham and all classes of trains could be seen. At Small Heath we could see through trains on both pairs of running lines and in between these trains passing by, we could watch the shunting that took place as Up trains were remarshalled in the sidings close to our vantage point. The starting point for Down trains was a little further away, but still visible from where we were standing.

Another form of activity was visits to engine sheds; usually organised by a local railway club using a motor coach to get to our destinations. While I enjoyed these visits, I always felt they were rushed. I would have rather seen fewer depots and spent more time looking at what was there. It did seem as if the vast majority of my colleagues just wanted to tick off as many numbers of engines as they could before rushing off to the next destination. Much later, in the summer of 1964, I was able to do the job properly. Circumstances at work allowed me to visit about fifty engine sheds during the course of a few weeks, mostly, but not all, ex LMS depots. I was able to wander round, talking to staff and noting and photographing what I saw, but only after I had obtained permission from the man in charge, explaining that I was an ex-engineman who knew how to behave in a locomotive shed.

I suppose it was inevitable that after a couple of dead end jobs, I would work on the railway. After a brief spell at Tyseley, I joined the LMS at Saltley motive power depot just prior to nationalisation. This consummated my lifelong love affair with the Victorian steam railway in all its forms. My work was far ranging but most of all I enjoyed my time in the Evesham link, a story that has been recounted elsewhere. (*An Illustrated History of the Ashchurch To Barnt Green Line - The Evesham Route*, Oxford Publishing Company, 2002) By 1955 however, it had become very clear to me that my boyhood ideals about a career on the railway were being tarnished. The status of enginemen had been eroded and the railway unions were against change. Notwithstanding the 1955 Modernisation Plan, the government was investing far more in roads rather than railways. While my interest remained undiminished, I could see that the writing was on the wall for the railway system of which I was a part.

Sitting on the footsteps of a goods brake van at Washwood Heath Down Sidings on a warm Spring day I contemplated my future and resolved to seek a career in sales, but to retain my interest in railways as a hobby. This would take the form of models, which I had been making for several years and in collecting photographs, books and other written material. A few years later in 1962 my first article was published and forty years on, I still am active in this field.

The acceleration of interest and involvement in the hobby began in the early 1960s when I ceased to be a loner and found that it was more rewarding to be part of a group of like-minded individuals. In 1963 I was a founder member of the LMS Society and my interest in detailed historical research began in earnest. Generally it was the demands of model making that set the course and direction for the research and in due course I came into contact with a number of people who were able to assist me in various ways. I would like to take this opportunity to record my debt to people like, H C Casserley, A G Ellis, J E Kite, R E Lacy, W O Steel, D Tee and K C Woodhead, all sadly no longer with us, who, in various ways, were of immense help and influenced my thoughts and my approach to railway history and research.

There is one other person who has provided a major stimulus to my researches, Dieter Hopkin, Head of Department, Library & Archive Collections at the National Railway Museum. During the course of a conversation a few years ago he said something to the effect that, 'if your generation do not sort out the shoe boxes, then the next one may find the task is beyond them'. Later I was to encounter the words of an American modeller and publisher, Vane Jones, who said, 'Knowledge is of no value unless it is shared with others'. His words sum up my sentiments. Therefore I would like to offer this book as a contribution towards the task of sorting out the shoebox of train operation and sharing my knowledge with my fellow modellers.

If the central theme of this book, that the operation of model railways should be based on the operating practice of the real thing, is taken up by modellers, it will add a different dimension to the construction and enjoyment of model railways. It is time that as much attention is given to accurately replicating the operating practices of the steam railway as has hitherto been reserved for other aspects of the hobby, such as the modelling of locomotives

and rolling stock. If this book contributes to this process, then it will have been worthwhile.

In the course of researching and writing this book, I have had great encouragement and assistance from many friends and colleagues. In particular I would like to acknowledge the help that I have received from John Edgington, whose comments and judgement I value immensely. Tony Overton, has drawn some of the diagrams reproduced in the pages which follow and, at the same time, made some very helpful suggestions about many aspects of signalling. It has also been a pleasure to work once again with Tony Wright, that master of the difficult art of model railway photography, whose splendid pictures enhance many of the pages of this book.

All the photographs used in the book are from the author's collection, unless otherwise stated.

Bob Essery
Rolleston on Dove
January 2003

Below: **Although I am not part of this group, this view, taken at Bletchley on the 25th May 1946, shows members of the Birmingham section of the Railway Correspondence and Travel Society, together with the transport that was used for shed visits at this period. There is not one anorak in sight and virtually all of the party are wearing ties!** G S Lloyd

Bottom: **The exterior of Small Heath & Sparkbrook station in the early years of British Railway's ownership, note that the word 'Great' in Great Western has been obliterated! This is a place that holds many happy memories for me and where my serious study of railways began. The photographer is standing on the pavement of Golden Hillock Road with the bridge wall behind him. It was over this bridge that my serious railway observations began.**

SETTING THE SCENE

Railway modellers will often talk about operation, but generally without explaining what they mean. If you were to put a number of them into a room and to ask them to describe the meaning of the words, model railway operation, there would be almost as many explanations as there were modellers present. This was certainly what transpired when I canvassed the views of a number of my modelling friends, not surprisingly there wasn't a consensus that agreed or defined the word.

To some, operation is all about a timetable of train movements designed to suit a particular model railway. It could be described as a form of jigsaw with the various train movements representing pieces that, when locked together, go to make up a complete picture. Others may look at the way the locomotives and the trains move on the layouts, not dissimilar to dancers on a stage where their movements must correspond to the orders of the choreographer who, in railway terms, is the signalman or traffic controller. Another viewpoint might suggest that the correct composition of the trains was the all-important feature to be reproduced. Others could place the emphasis upon the signalling systems and their operation, requiring full interlocking and other features.

In many respects this diversity of opinion is useful because it has enabled me to provide my own definition, to say what I believe we mean, or perhaps what we ought to mean by model railway operation and to describe the various ingredients that go to make the complete picture. While I do not expect everyone to agree with me, if this book helps, even in a small way, to stimulate debate and leads to an improvement in the standards of operation, on model railways, then the work will have been worthwhile. More importantly perhaps, it may

prompt modellers to seek their inspiration from the prototype, rather than to copy their fellow modellers, as far as layout design is concerned.

It is inevitable that modellers will always be influenced by the work of other modellers. I have had the good fortune to have been involved with two layouts which have had a significant influence on aspects of the hobby. Both layouts were inspired, one directly the other indirectly, by the work of Peter Gomm. In the early 1960s Peter built an EM layout that was in the form of an oval. At each end of the front of the layout there were two double junctions, whilst at the rear there were a number of parallel sidings to hold the trains. I am not sure if we would have described this arrangement in those days as the fiddle sidings, but that is what they would be called today. This layout, or rather its concept, provided the inspiration for David Jenkinson's EM layout, Garsdale Road, and that railway and its operating concept inspired the design of Heckmondwike, built by the North London Group to P4 standards. Neither Garsdale Road nor Heckmondwike's track layouts were identical to Peter's railway, but the operational concept was.

Whilst there is nothing wrong in a modeller seeking inspiration from other modellers' work, in my view, it is always better to base a new layout on a suitable prototype rather than on other layouts. If the modeller does his research properly he will ensure that the design he builds is in accordance with real practice. By adopting this approach he will avoid repeating mistakes that other modellers may have made, if he has based his layout on their work. The oft heard term, modeller's licence, could be interpreted as meaning, 'I know that it is wrong, but I am too idle to get it right and most folk won't notice anyway!' My dear friend, the late John Horton, used to say, 'Seek inspiration from the prototype, the Victorian engineers who built the railways encountered these problems at a scale of 12 inches to 1 foot and they solved them. All that

you have to do is to adapt their solutions to your model, built to the scale of your choosing'. This advice has proved to be very sound indeed.

My first attempts to build a model railway dated from 1946. By then I have saved enough money to buy some second hand, pre-war, Trix Twin equipment, though I considered it to be very unrealistic. This was exchanged for some pre-war second-hand 00 material; one freelance locomotive lettered LMS, about ten goods wagons, and a few points. I was able to obtain some track parts from Hamblings, a track gauge, rail, I think it was brass, and brass sleepers. My first soldering iron was not even electric; it was heated in a coal fire. The system was three rail and after a while I was able to obtain a power unit, but I had to make my controller using brass studs, which were mounted onto a thin board that was connected to resistance wire and a control handle that altered

Bottom left: **This picture, taken in 1962, shows the engine shed on my first EM layout. This was a portable affair, which explains the join line between the base of the shed and the baseboard. I am not sure what the large mound at the far right of the picture is meant to represent 40 years later, The siding leading to the simple coal stage has room for several coal wagons as well as the locomotive at the coaling stage. There are fire irons on the ground and the corrugated bin is for smokebox ash and char. Inspection and disposal pits can also be seen. The 2-6-2T engine belonged to my friend Derrick Smith, as indeed did the two visiting GWR coal wagons.** Tony Thatcher

Opposite page, top: **If a modeller wishes to build a fictional layout it makes sense to create a story and to place the railway into the British railway system. This map, drawn by Barry Lane, shows my original thoughts for Dewsbury. I think that it is important to clearly establish what is beyond the area actually modelled. In my case, the railway begins when southbound trains emerge from the tunnel and ends when they pass under Wynne Street road bridge to the south of the engine shed.**

Opposite page, bottom: **This picture dates from 1995 and shows Midland Railway 4-4-0 No 2193 on the Up main line at Dewsbury station. This posed photograph was taken at an exhibition and for some reason we used this top link engine to work a cattle train, an unusual but not unknown arrangement. It would be more usual to have a cattle wagon included as part of a passenger train, subject to the wagon being equipped with acceptable brakes and couplings, as seen in a picture on page 65.** Tony Wright

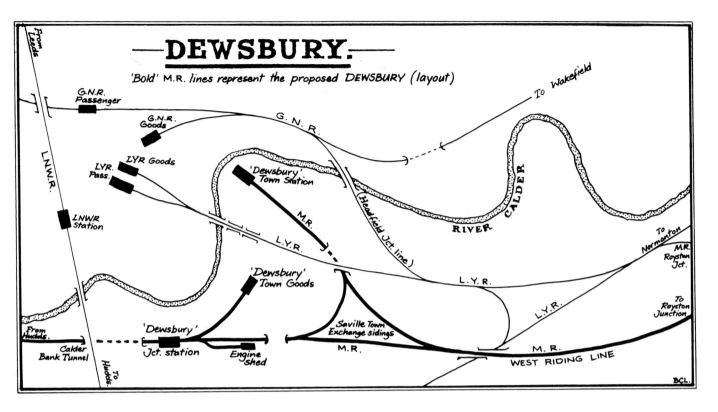

DEWSBURY.

'Bold' M.R. lines represent the proposed DEWSBURY (layout)

the power output. Needless to say it did not work very well. I built a second locomotive using a ready-made chassis purchased from Hamblings and also built a small terminus station. However, by 1951, I decided that maybe Gauge 0 would be a better proposition.

The 00 material was sold and I started again, working to Gauge 0 coarse standard. The layout was little more than a portable test track, an oval with a loop and two sidings. Motive power was one steam and one electric locomotive, and by now I had a proper controller. I enjoyed building the track, cast metal chairs, through which the rail was threaded, the chairs then being nailed to sleepers. By the beginning of 1954, the space that I had for storing my models was wanted for other purposes so everything was sold.

In 1946 I had started to purchase magazines, both modelling and prototype. In those days paper was rationed and you had to wait for someone to stop taking their order before you could obtain a copy of certain magazines. It was almost a case of dead man's shoes. When each volume was complete, I used to have the copies bound and this marked the beginning of my collection of books that has grown ever since. Later I added photographs, drawings and official railway publications to the collection.

Model making restarted in 1956 and I adopted 00 two-rail. My prime interest was scratch building wagons. My layout was just a portable shunting yard, three sidings and a shunting neck. In 1960 I was persuaded that EM was far more accurate than 00 and I changed to that standard. By 1971 I became convinced that P4 standards were the ultimate in 4mm scale. For the next nine years I was mostly involved with the North London Group and the Heckmondwike layout, but when that layout went to the National Railway Museum, it was time for a change again.

In 1980 I returned to Gauge 0 adopting Finescale standards but in time I felt that I had made a mistake, so in 1989 I became one of the founder members of the Scale 7 Group and I have never regretted this change. Modelling scales and standards are a personal choice. My desire has been to produce a model railway that is as accurate as I can make it and accurate dimensions are a fundamental part of this approach. Therefore, irrespective of whatever scales or standards you adopt, much of what I have so say in this book about operation, will apply to your layout.

What is essential for realistic railway operation in model form is to slavishly follow scale standards. Although I have advocated scale rather than model standards for almost 30 years, they are not essential for a layout whose main function is to represent operational practice in an accurate fashion. What scale standards offer is the visual harmony that cannot be achieved with a modelling standard. The most popular modelling standard in the United Kingdom is 00 where the track is built to a scale of 3.5mm to one foot and the super-

structure of the locomotives and rolling stock and indeed everything else, to a scale of 4mm to the foot. This at once gives rise to a problem with the layout of the track. As the aim of this book is to link the model railway to the real thing, let us use the proper railway terms when discussing this problem.

In the language of the railway, the space between two lines of rail is called the four foot, that between two tracks is known as the six foot. With 00 and indeed to a lesser or similar degree with the other modelling standards, the six foot, has to be increased in order to accommodate the wider than scale stock. This is most apparent on curves and while most modellers would not worry about this it simply means that where tracks come together at points and crossings the geometry has to be altered and a totally accurate scale model of that section of track cannot be built. One good example of this is a three way point. While a representation can be modelled, an accurate scale model is probably not possible, unless modellers use scale standards.

As far as track layouts are concerned, take heart from the following example from the real world, one of many hundreds if not thousands which could be quoted, from a report of a Board of Trade inspecting officer. On 16th July 1900 Major General Hutchinson reported that, 'following his inspection of, alterations and new connections in the main line at Whitacre, he would not approve the new work. He required the Midland Railway to provide interlocked safety points on a siding to protect the Hampton passenger line and that No 31 disc (ground signal), should lock No 26 points.' The railway company had no option other than to comply. Although his handwriting was awful, it was all written in beautiful, if somewhat stilted English. The point I seek to make is that if the railway companies did not always get it right, what chance do modellers have?

The reality of our quest for operational accuracy is often further compromised by the requirement that a layout should be portable. This is something which the designers of the Victorian prototypes did not have to concern themselves with and indeed, if a layout is never going to leave its home, this problem does not arise. However, if a layout is to be built to go on to the exhibition circuit, there is often the view that something must be seen running all the time. I am tempted to ask why this should be as even the busiest of British main lines do not have trains constantly in view. The problem stems from the demands of the exhibition circuit to keep the customers happy with something happening all the time. The solution is a layout based upon an oval where the trains can go round and round. There are places in Great Britain where this does occur the Circle Line on the London Underground being probably the best known.

Therefore the builder of a new layout needs to decide if he is in the entertainment business, in which case a circular layout, or something based upon a round and round layout, is ideal.

The alternative is to build a section of railway in model form that may be used as a continuous run but really operates as a through line. Railways ran from A to B, with junctions that lead to C, D, I believe that our models should reflect this approach.

Perhaps I should close this section by describing my own model railway. When it is complete it will be of a length of main line that emerges from beneath an overbridge, passes a small locomotive shed, which serves the local traffic needs, runs through a station and into a tunnel. It is point to point with cassette boards at each end of the line. Between the station and the engine shed there is a junction that leads to a goods station, which is fairly extensive. The operating potential is considerable, trains that pass through, trains that attach or detach traffic at the goods station, trains that run to and from the goods station, light engine movements to and from the goods station and the marshalling yards, which are off stage. All main line movements are controlled in accordance with the absolute block system and the points and signals are fully interlocked. A lot of activity takes place, even though the trains do not go round and round and round. The truth is that when this layout is operating, it will be a lot more like the real railway than many of the models which are seen at exhibitions, where a succession of trains run past at speed, operating at a frequency which bear little relation to the reality of the actuality of the steam railway in its heyday.

For example, recently at an exhibition, I saw a large 4mm layout with a through passenger station with two loops and a tunnel mouth close to the end of the station. A goods in one of the loops was given the road and ran into the tunnel. Within seconds the main line signals were cleared and an express hurtled into the tunnel. There should have been a big bang as the express ran into the rear of the freight train. The operators were trying to entertain the public with constant train movements, in my case they failed!

Opposite page:

Top: **The original model of Dewsbury station did not have a bay platform for passenger trains. The line where the inspection coach is standing is the end of the goods station shunting neck, which is why it is fenced off from the platform. The rebuilt Dewsbury has a cross-over between the main lines, this enables the train that works between the junction and town station to use this bay, now that the fence has been taken down. No 2440 was built by Geoff Holt and in this picture, it was hauling a rake of Ken Cottle's carriages.**

Bottom: **This picture, like the one above, was taken at an exhibition and shows another of Ken Cottle's locomotives and carriages.** Both Tony Wright

THE MODELLER'S OVERVIEW

Most railway modellers would say that their major problem in fulfilling their modelling ambitions is lack of space. Therefore let us explore, in a philosophical mood, some of the pros and cons of space, or rather the lack of it. Within an area, for example a room with fixed walls that cannot be moved or tunnelled through, a layout of a given size can be built in that most popular of scales, 4mm to the foot,

00 gauge. If a modeller decides that he needs more space he can use a smaller scale, 3 or 2mm scale. The later is half the size of 4mm scale and if adopted it will allow rather more railway to be built in the area. On the other hand 4mm scale may be considered too small for the models he wishes to build and his thoughts turn towards S Gauge or O Gauge.

In my experience most modellers often try to cram in too much railway within the space available to them. Years ago with 7mm scale, or as it was always called, O Gauge, it was not uncommon to build layouts on two or more levels in order to get the length of run the

owner required. This was particularly true for modellers who used clockwork motors to drive their locomotives.

The wheel and track standards adopted at the start of the twentieth century, which is when the hobby of model railways really began, were rather coarse. They allowed trains to run round sharp curves that would be quite unacceptable by today's standards. For example a two foot radius in 0 Gauge was considered generous and some track formations used even tighter curves. Many years were to pass before the move towards scale standards began, but when they came there was a price to be paid. The closer the wheel and track standards are to scale, the wider radius the curves must be. Today we have three groups of wheel and track standards. The early standards date from the beginning of 0 Gauge and although they were later modified they were still very coarse.

A similar approach to wheel and track standards was used with the introduction of 00/H0

Left: **This picture has been included as evidence that I do practice what I preach concerning modelling standards. It was taken during the first half of 1990 and shows the first Scale 7 track that I built for Dewsbury, a trailing cross over from the Down main line (nearest to the camera) to the Up shunting line, with a slip connection to the Up main line. The crossing angle is 1 in 7 and the track was constructed from Slaters track parts using Adrian Testers cast chairs.** Tony Wright

Left: **This is one answer to the space problem. Shortly before I started to write this book, I built the track for a minimum space shunting layout that is designed to be operated by 0-4-0T or 0-6-0T engines. You do not have to run large passenger engines if you want a realistic model railway and using small engines like this, placing them in a model of a dockside or in an industrial railway setting, can be quite delightful. The late John Horton rebuilt this locomotive to Scale 7 standards. No 1323A was one of several of my Finescale locomotives which benefited from his work. Although only fitted with a RG4 motor, the locomotive is quite powerful and can easily haul 40 wagon trains, rather more than can be accommodated on this particular layout.** Tony Wright

Above: **Although some express trains were indeed lengthy, this was not always the case. The traffic carried over some lines did not require long trains. This picture, dating from the early post-grouping period, shows an ex Great Central 4-4-2 No 1089 working what the photographer described as a Down Nottingham to Marylebone express. That an express working could consist of** only four coaches train, makes this point admirably.

Below: **Described as an, 'Up Manchester slow at Charwelton water troughs', this picture of LNER D10 Director class 4-4-0 No 5437 Prince George, shows the locomotive hauling a train that appears to be made up of seven vehicles. Apart from** wishing to contrast it with the picture above, the slow train is longer than the express, I also want to draw attention to the leading vehicles. Many modellers tend to make the composition of their passenger trains too tidy and too uniform, the reality on the full size railway was often very different.

Above: **Not all the goods trains recorded during the age of steam were lengthy, as this picture of an ex-Caledonian Railway 0-6-0 No 57642 at Beauly in July 1954, demonstrates. The train consists of only three loaded open wagons.** A G Ellis

during the 1920s and after the Second World War with the arrival of the TT and N gauges. Standards were coarse to begin with. Later improvements saw the introduction of finer wheel and track standards and finally, beginning with 4mm scale, with the development of what was to become known as P4, a true scale standard emerged in the late 1960s. It is important for modellers to remember that the wheel and track standard chosen has a major bearing upon the amount of space required for a given track formation.

To obtain more space the easiest solution is to work to a smaller scale, but this reduces the mass of the model and, in my view, the smaller the scale the more difficult it becomes to obtain good running. There are two possible approaches to the question of space. The first is to reduce your ambitions in terms of train length and the second is to go back in time as far as the date of your model is concerned. From the earliest days of the hobby, the trade has often concentrated upon the latest and most modern examples of motive power and rolling stock in service. The problem is that modern stock, in this regard we have to consider post grouping as being modern, was bigger than what had gone before. By the late

1930s an express passenger train, and there was no real change in size from this point onwards, was long. For example, a typical 4-6-2 tender locomotive will be over 70ft in length and a 15 coach train, made up of a mixture of 57/60ft carriages, would add another 915 or so feet in length. In 7mm scale such a formation would take up around 23 feet, while in 4mm scale the train would be just over 13ft long. A model 2-8-0 freight engine will need to have at least 25 wagons behind its tender to represent a reasonably sized main line goods train. If we use 17ft 6in, the post 1923 standard for goods stock, as being the average length of a wagon or van, something like 8ft in 4mm and 14ft in 7mm scale will be needed to accommodate a train of this length.

If we consider the first option, namely to reduce the train length, then there are numerous possibilities. Industrial sites and works sidings, branch and secondary lines all spring to mind. The problem with country branch lines is that generally they were laid out with a generous use of land, so while they do not attract as much traffic or the lengthy trains seen on the main lines, the track layout was often spread over a wide area. This is not what we seek in our search to save space. One alternative is to model an urban terminus or a through station. Urban termini were generally in confined spaces, hemmed in by retaining walls or on embankments and as such they are usually more economical in the use of land than country stations.

My preferred option is to go back in time to an era when everything was smaller. Not only did the Edwardian period represent in many respects the heyday of the British steam railway, from a modeller's point of view, the trains were not as long. An express passenger train, hauled by a 4-4-0, with say five bogie coaches and a six-wheel passenger brake van, will measure almost 8ft in 7mm scale and just over 4ft in 4mm scale. A 0-6-0 goods locomotive with a train of 12 wagons and a brake van, will take up less than 7ft in 7mm scale and about 4ft in 4mm scale. In this era everything was smaller. The average wagon length at this time was about 15ft and coaches were 50ft or less.

Shorter trains also mean that the distance between stations can be reduced and while the rules about the positioning of signals should not be broken, it is possible to tighten up the distances between stations if the modeller does not insist on reproducing the post 1930 main line scene. What I find most encouraging today is the imagination displayed by modellers when they have little space at their disposal. I hope that as a wider understanding of various aspects of full size railway operating practice becomes better known, then even more imaginative layouts will be constructed. There will of course be some modellers who have deep pockets and plenty of space, in which case the main line, with its full-length trains, will not be out of place and presents a glorious spectacle.

Opposite page, top: **This view illustrates the problem which the length of main line goods trains can present for the modeller. Taken at Beattock during the early years of the last century, the locomotive in charge of the train is a Caledonian 812 class 0-6-0. The leading vehicles in the train are interesting. The first is an open carriage truck, the second a L&NWR covered carriage truck, with doors at the end as well as along the sides. The third vehicle demonstrates the way in which brake levers were positioned on many vehicles at this time. When the railway companies were persuaded that they needed to equip their wagons with brakes, at first they fitted the brake lever to one side of the vehicle only. As a result many shunters were injured when ducking between wagons to reach the brake lever on the other side of the vehicle. Board of Trade pressure to reduce such accidents led to the companies fitting the brake lever to both sides. For a while the levers were both fitted at the same end. Eventually the companies were required to construct their wagons with the brake lever to the right hand of a man when he faced the wagon from the side. The last examples of wagons with the earlier types of brake gear were still in service until the late 1930s. If a modeller is working in the pre-grouping period this is something which has to be considered. The positioning of brake levers on wagons at that time being different from that which pertained in the closing decades of the age of steam. The period being modelled can thus have a bearing on something as basic as the type of brake gear seen on the wagons on the layout.**

Opposite page, bottom: **This picture was probably taken in the late 1930s and shows an ex L&NWR 0-6-0 'Coal' engine, No 8290, near Garstang in Lancashire. This working is a stopping freight train, note the target board with the number 15 on the right hand tender lamp iron. It was not uncommon to carry a target board, which gave the trip number, where the locomotive headlamp should have been, an unwritten rule followed by firemen perhaps. It is notable that even though it is on a main line, the train is short and the locomotive is running tender first. Out and back trip workings with tender engines often entailed tender first working. If the weather was bad the storm sheet, seen rolled up under the cab roof, would be used to protect the engine crew.**

Above: **Modellers are often criticised for the severity of the curves on their layouts in comparison with the prototype. However, sharp curves did exist on full size railways as this picture demonstrates. The location is the 1 in 60 gradient into Oban, the locomotives in charge of this half day excursion from Dundee in August 1937, are** 0-6-0 No 17904 piloting 4-6-0 No 14691 *Brodie Castle*.

Below: **Another potential solution for those with a limited amount of space for a layout, is to look to the world of the light railway. Although I have never built such a model myself, I freely admit there is a fascination** about this type of railway and can understand why so many enthusiasts are drawn towards them. A model based upon the Wisbech to Upwell line, seen here, would not occupy too much space and would certainly create a lot of interest.

THE ELEMENTS OF MODEL RAILWAY OPERATION

The operational activities discussed in these pages relate to those which were part of the traditional Victorian steam railway. Many of these operating practices were defined in all their essential details by 1889 and continued, with little change, until 1968 when steam traction ceased on British Railways. Whilst residual practices from the steam era continued for some years after the end of steam, as the equipment used gradually changed, so did the operating practices. One obvious example of this was the move away from unbraked to fully braked freight trains. Therefore this book is about what came before the end of steam and not the what came afterwards. So many points of difference could be noted between the two eras that it would be impossible to include them all in one volume, even if I were qualified to write about them, which I am not.

Model railways come in many forms. One person may wish to have little more than a setting through which trains can be run whenever they feel like running them, while another may want to operate a complicated and detailed timetable. I can enjoy both, but my preference

is for the latter. If we want to create such a timetable for a fictitious location, we have to do some careful planning .

Railways were built to carry traffic and the track formation reflected both the type and volume of traffic that was to be carried. Signals were placed to control the traffic over the track formation. Their location and the type used could vary according to the period and the volume of traffic they had to control. If traffic increased, additional lines could be built in order to cope with it, but if the traffic decreased, the facilities were reduced and perhaps eventually, as happened so often in the 1960s and 70s, a line would be closed. Therefore, a modeller planning a railway based upon a fictitious location should begin by deciding what sort of traffic he wishes to carry over his railway.

The period to be modelled should also be considered with care. For example, some modellers will say that they are modelling the XYZ Railway between 1920 and 1940. Of course this is quite impossible if total accuracy is your aim. Some stock that was running in the early 1920s would, in reality, have been scrapped by the start of the next decade and could not have been seen alongside stock introduced in the 1930s. Apart from the lifespan of the various pieces of equipment, the painting styles also varied over the years. However, if your aim is

to provide a representation of your chosen railway over a number of years, it is better not to be too specific and to accept that your model may display inconsistencies.

Even this this approach can have its drawbacks. A good example of this relates to distant signals which will be found on most model railways. Everybody knows that today the semaphore arms of distant signals are painted yellow on the front face. However, this only became the case from the mid 1920s onwards.

Below: **Dating from around 1893, this view of Barton station at Hereford, shows GWR signals and a MR passenger train consisting of a 0-4-4 tank loco and a rake of six wheel vehicles. The entire train, including the locomotive, is only about the length of three and a half modern bogie coaches, which graphically illustrates my point that if space for your layout is limited, consider modelling an earlier period of railway history. The distinctive early semaphore signals, seen here, would also add distinction to a layout of this era. Also of note is the wagon turntable in the foreground, something which would not normally have been seen at an important station like this, in later years.**

Opposite page, top: **On first glance this view of St Pancras station in London could well date from the LMS era because of the preponderance of LMS locomotives . However, closer examination reveals a coach in two tone livery, BR carmine and cream, and that the locomotive on the extreme right hand side of the picture is a British Railways built Class 5MT 4-6-0. In the course of researching various projects over the years, I have looked at a surprising number of photographs which have come with no dating information at all. I include this picture of the Midland London terminus not in the hope that it will inspire someone to rush off and start building a model of it, but merely to highlight one of the hazards which can accompany research in the archives.** P Ransome-Wallis

Above: **The pictures on this page provide an interesting contrast between the express trains of two different eras. The pre-1914 view of GNR bogie single No 270 with its short train of mostly six wheel vehicles is a world away from the other view, taken only about a quarter of a century later. The finish on the GNR locomotive is quite superb. A study of a range of photographs of working locomotives from this era will confirm that such standards of presentation were the norm and not the exception. One other point of interest for** potential modellers of this era in the photograph, is the ballast. This was often much finer at this period than it was in later years and was frequently laid over the top of the sleepers.

Below: **If I was asked to nominate one symbol to represent the railways in the 1930s it would be the streamlined trains operated by the LMS and the LNER. In this 1939 picture we see the Down Coronation Scot hauled by Princes Coronation class 4-6-2 No 6229 *Duchess of Hamilton*.**

Opposite page, bottom: **Subtle changes in the landscape of the real railway can be perceived in the study of period photographs and easily recreated on a model as this 1962 view of Evesham station demonstrates. What was once a through line, in the foreground, has been truncated with a buffer stop to make it a mere siding. Changes to long established layouts such as this, were often cost savings measures in response to the loss of traffic to road transport at this time. The line of cars in the foreground is another hint of this major change in national transport habits.** M Mensing

Prior to then, they were painted red, with only a notch cut into the end of the signal to distinguish them from a home signal. Achieving historical accuracy is not easy and there are many traps for the unwary modeller.

For some reason many modellers seem to prefer to invent a location from scratch. This makes their research even more complex and difficult. I would urge those starting to build a new model railway, to base this on an actual prototype, on the grounds that it is so much easier to build a model of what existed than to invent one! A compromise is to build a model of a line that was proposed but not completed. It depends to some extent on one's attitude to research, whether it is a chore or a pleasure. I have widened my knowledge of railways in general considerably whilst researching Midland Railway practice for a model. I have also learnt something about the practice of other companies and how this varied from what the Midland did. Whilst some modellers enjoy research others, I suspect, use the search for that final elusive detail as an excuse to never actually build anything!

When planning a layout based upon a fictitious location, the first essential is to resolve what traffic is to be run over it, in other words, what was the reason for building this imaginary line. The next requirement is the track formation and its associated signalling. This must conform to the statutory requirements of the period depicted by the model.

The nature of signalling changed over the years. Some modellers of layouts based upon the pre-grouping period tend to signal their layouts using a 1950/60s approach. As a result their models present a somewhat over signalled appearance. Further changes to signalling also took place when automatic and colour light signals were introduced, so while the principle of block working remained, the

way this was implemented varied and it is this type of detail that helps to set the date of a model railway.

In order to illustrate this point, I have asked Tony Overton to prepare a set of drawings which show how the layout of tracks and signals at a fictitious location, which we will call, Somewhere Junction, might have evolved over the years. Though not based upon a specific location, many elements in the design have been taken from actual stations and the layout illustrated is firmly grounded in reality. The three drawings on the page opposite, show how the layout could have changed over a 50 year period. They are dated 1880, 1914 and 1930 respectively.

In 1880 (left opposite) this main line junction was worked on the absolute block system. There were Up and Down lines with two lie-byes and a large private siding on the Up side. Access to the private siding from the Down main line was via the points R, worked from the signal box, and by hand signals. From the Up main line, the siding was reached by points worked from an independent lever frame, which is in the block section. This arrangement of a lever frame in the block section was not uncommon at this time. With this arrangement it would be normal for signals A and B to be in the off position. These were controlled from the lever stage. When a train was required to set back into the private sidings, the guard would stop the train when the brakevan was clear of the points and go to the lever stage. He would return the signals A and B to the on position and the train could be set back into the private siding. When the work was complete the train would return to the main line, the guard would reset the points and return the signals to the off position and the train would depart. By this date distant signals were erected at the braking distance from the home

signal. It was then usual to have arms that applied to different routes on the same post.

By around 1914, (centre opposite), the number of signals had increased and moves that had, in the past, been controlled by hand signals were now controlled by fixed signals. The most obvious change is that the lever stage on the Up main line, has been brought inside station limits. This has occurred through signal E, the Up starting signal, being repositioned beyond the lever stage. The lever stage is now bolt locked and is no longer independent. Despite what has happened here, it was still not uncommon to find independent lever stages, within block sections, into the 1960s. Exit from the private sidings is by a ground disc worked from the lever stage. Due to the increase in traffic since 1880, a new signal box has been opened in the Up direction and this new box's distant signal is on the same post as Somewhere Junction's Up starting signal. In the Down direction the setting back move into the Down lie-bye is controlled by fixed signals and not hand signalled.

By 1930, (right opposite), there have been further changes to the point and signalling arrangements at Somewhere Junction. The Down lie-bye has become a loop for goods trains and the disc has been replaced by a running line signal. The sidings on the Up side have been greatly enlarged and the lever stage has been removed. Note the way the Up siding line has been slued around the signal post to maintain the required clearance, a common feature when additional lines were laid outside of the main lines.

The locomotives and rolling stock used can also make a statement as to the accuracy of a model. Remember the cascade principal which applied across the railway system. Locomotives displaced from important main line work were often to be found working on branch lines and coaches that were originally built for service on main line express trains could end their days as part of branch line sets. There can be no doubt that to study the prototype is by far the best approach and the temptation to buy the latest kit, just because you like it, should be resisted until you establish if it will fit into your scheme of things.

Left: **This picture, taken during the first years of grouping at the former MR St Thomas station in Swansea, tells an interesting story. To the right of the picture are a number of old ex-North London Railway carriages. New LMS coaches have replaced these on services into Broad Street station in London and on the principle of cascading older stock which has been replaced, they have been sent to this LMS outpost in South Wales for further duties, probably on workmens' trains. The locomotive in the picture is 0-4-4T No 1424, and the first four vehicles behind it are ex-MR non corridor coaches.**

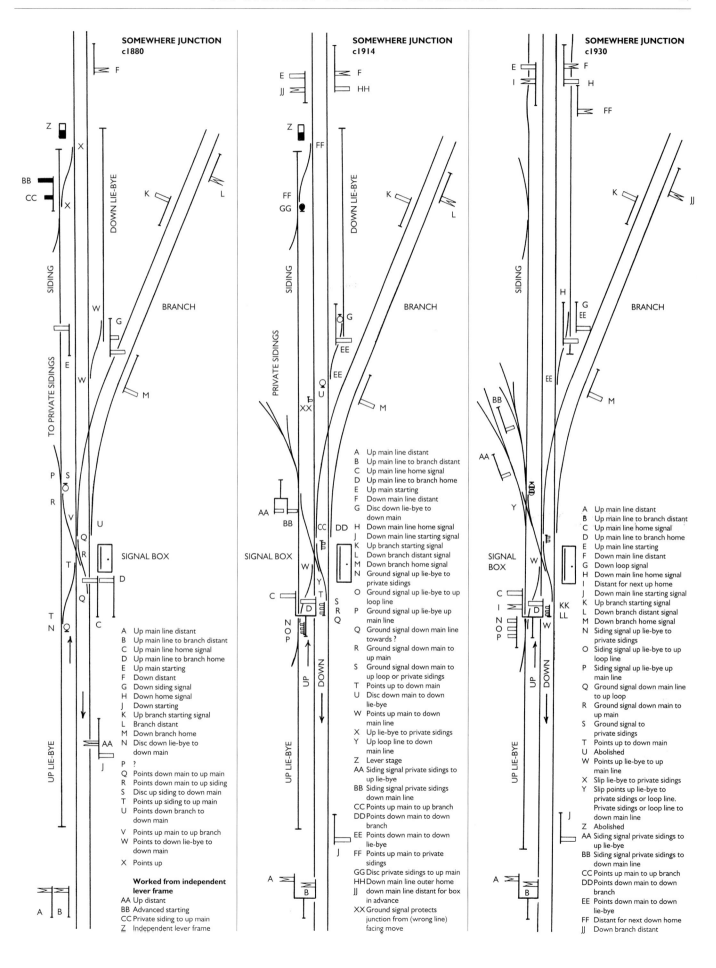

SOMEWHERE JUNCTION
c1880

A   Up main line distant
B   Up main line to branch distant
C   Up main line home signal
D   Up main line to branch home
E   Up main starting
F   Down distant
G   Down siding signal
H   Down home signal
J   Down starting
K   Up branch starting signal
L   Branch distant
M   Down branch home
N   Disc down lie-bye to
     down main
P   ?
Q   Points down main to up main
R   Points down main to up siding
S   Disc up siding to down main
T   Points up siding to up main
U   Points down branch to
     down main
V   Points up main to up branch
W   Points to down lie-bye to
     down main
X   Points up

**Worked from independent
lever frame**
AA Up distant
BB Advanced starting
CC Private siding to up main
Z   Independent lever frame

SOMEWHERE JUNCTION
c1914

A   Up main line distant
B   Up main line to branch distant
C   Up main line home signal
D   Up main line to branch home
E   Up main starting
F   Down main line distant
G   Disc down lie-bye to
     down main
H   Down main line home signal
J   Down main line starting signal
K   Up branch starting signal
L   Down branch distant signal
M   Down branch home signal
N   Ground signal up lie-bye to
     private sidings
O   Ground signal up lie-bye to up
     loop line
P   Ground signal up lie-bye up
     main line
Q   Ground signal down main line
     towards ?
R   Ground signal down main to
     up main
S   Ground signal down main to
     up loop or private sidings
T   Points up to down main
U   Disc down main to down
     lie-bye
W   Points up main to down
     main line
X   Up lie-bye to private sidings
Y   Up loop line to down
     main line
Z   Lever stage
AA Siding signal private sidings to
     up lie-bye
BB Siding signal private sidings
     down main line
CC Points up main to up branch
DD Points down main to down
     branch
EE Points down main to down
     lie-bye
FF Points up main to private
     sidings
GG Disc private sidings to up main
HH Down main line outer home
JJ   down main line distant for box
     in advance
XX Ground signal protects
     junction from (wrong line)
     facing move

SOMEWHERE JUNCTION
c1930

A   Up main line distant
B   Up main line to branch distant
C   Up main line home signal
D   Up main line to branch home
E   Down main line distant
F   Down main line distant
G   Down loop signal
H   Down main line home signal
I   Distant for next up home
J   Down main line starting signal
K   Up branch starting signal
L   Down branch distant signal
M   Down branch home signal
N   Siding signal up lie-bye to
     private sidings
O   Siding signal up lie-bye to up
     loop line
P   Siding signal up lie-bye up
     main line
Q   Ground signal down main line
     to up loop
R   Ground signal down main to
     up main
S   Ground signal to
     private sidings
T   Points up to down main
U   Abolished
W   Points up lie-bye to up
     main line
X   Slip lie-bye to private sidings
Y   Slip points up lie-bye to
     private sidings or loop line.
     Private sidings or loop line to
     down main line
Z   Abolished
AA Siding signal private sidings to
     up lie-bye
BB Siding signal private sidings to
     down main line
CC Points up main to up branch
DD Points down main to down
     branch
EE Points down main to down
     lie-bye
FF Distant for next down home
JJ   Down branch distant

RAILWAY LEGISLATION

From its very beginning a number of significant forces helped to mould the British railway system. One of these was competition from other forms of transport and among the railway companies themselves, however, one of the most important of these factors was the role of government and legislation which it imposed to control the activities of the companies and ensure basic standards of safety. An awareness of some of this railway legislation is important for the railway historian, but also for the modeller. For example, take the 1839 Railway Level Crossing Act which compelled the railways companies to erect and maintain gates at level crossings of public roadways and to employ a suitable person to open and shut the gates. This established the basic rules governing the crossing of a railway on the level. The Railway Regulation Act of 1842 extended these regulations and stipulated that level crossing gates were now to be kept constantly closed across the public road, when not required to be opened for road traffic, unless the Board of

Trade ordered otherwise. The gates were also to be constructed so as to fence in the line of railway at both ends of the public road. This act also provided that fences were to be erected and maintained alongside railways, every line now had to be fenced off from the public. No model of a railway is accurate without boundary fences of some kind thanks to this 160 year old piece of legislation.

I will briefly mention just two other pieces of nineteenth century railway legislation, both significant in very different ways. The Light Railways Act of 1896 gave the Board of Trade the power to license a railway company to construct or work any line or section of track as a light railway. This was defined as one where the load did not exceed 8 tons on any pair of wheels or where the speed did not exceed 25 miles per hour. This legislation gave rise to some of the more charming and quirkier parts of the British railway network. Models of light railways are not uncommon but anyone contemplating recreating one of these lines should familiarise themselves with the legislation under which the prototypes were regulated.

In railway terms, the fundamental law which defined basic operating practices for the

remaining 80 or so years of the steam era and beyond was the Regulation of Railways Act of 1889. This was the most important of all the Acts passed in relation to railways in the nineteenth century. It was a remarkably prompt response to the terrible Armagh accident on the Great Northern Railway of Ireland which occurred on 12th June of that year. This vividly highlighted the necessity for automatic continuous brakes and absolute block working. The Act required that all companies adopt the absolute block system on all passenger lines, that points and signals on all passenger lines were to be interlocked and all passenger trains had to be equipped with continuous brakes.

I have always regarded the provisions of the 1889 Act as being the line between the early years of development of railways and the railway which I knew some 50 or so years ago. It would not be incorrect to say that a railwayman who was familiar with the British railway scene post the 1889 legislation would be quite at home on the railways in 1950 or later. He would find that the engines and rolling stock were larger than he was used to and that they ran slightly more quickly, but the rules, regulations and equipment would not be alien to him.

Opposite page: **The axle loading restrictions in the 1896 Act meant that light railways were usually worked with small locomotives. This in turn meant that the weight of the rolling stock had to be in keeping with the power of the locomotives. In this view taken on of the Kelvedon & Tollesbury Light Railway in Essex, J67 class 0-6-0T No 68608, towers over its train.** J H Aston

Top: **One of the requirements of the 1839 Act was that level crossings should be provided with gates. This example at Irthlingboro, taken on the 3rd February 1934, shows the gates open for road traffic. Note the home signal protecting the gates and the barrow crossing, on the station side of the gates, between the Up and Down platforms.** H C Casserley

Centre: **Light railways were built where it would was thought that a normal standard gauge line, with all its construction and operating costs, would not have been viable. This picture, taken in April 1949, illustrates the terminus of the Mid Suffolk Light Railway at Laxfield. The platform height is low and the building have been cheaply constructed of corrugated iron.** W A Camwell

Bottom: **This view of North Staffordshire Railway 2-4-0T No 18 built in 1882, was taken before the locomotive was fitted with an automatic vacuum brake. At the date this picture was taken, the only brakes which could be applied to this train were the guard's handbrake and that on the engine. It was the lack of an automatic brake which caused the GNRI train, stalled on the incline outside Armagh station on 12th June 1889, to come to grief, leading to the death of 80 excursionists and compelling the government to act so quickly and decisively.**

TRACK FORMATION

Whilst I suspect that the majority of modellers would regard the locomotive as being the most important feature on their layouts, I have always taken the view that the most important part of a layout is the track and signals.

I like the expression, permanent way, which has something enduring or everlasting about it, to describe track . I think I can reasonably assume that readers of this book will be familiar with the various components that make up a length of permanent way such as rails, sleepers, chairs and fishplates. The type of permanent way used should be appropriate for the date of the model. For example, the use of flat bottom rail on a main line layout with a suggested date in the 1920s would be a glaring error.

In simple terms, lengths of permanent way can be divided into either passenger carrying or non-passenger carrying lines, sidings being classed within the latter category. Lines that are passed for passenger traffic can have different names such as main lines, passenger lines, fast lines, slow lines and relief lines. In stations, terms such as platform lines and bay lines may also be used. Lines intended for passenger traffic had to meet higher standards which were set originally by the Board of Trade and in later years, by the Ministry of Transport. Non passenger lines may be referred to as

goods lines, mineral lines, sidings, loops (though some loop lines maybe passed for passenger trains), shunting necks or headshunts. The last two terms refer to the same thing as does lie-byes, lay-bys or refuge sidings.

The earliest railways were either double or single line but as traffic increased additional tracks were often required. These additional lines could be built on either side of the existing lines. Other ways to increase the number of running lines included extending on both sides of the existing line or building lines that diverted away from the original line. Usually these deviation lines as they were called, were due to adverse gradients and could lead to some unusual track formations. Refuge sidings, many of which were later converted into loops, were added to allow faster moving trains to overtake slower traffic.

The track formation and the type of traffic which will use it influences the signalling required. The direction of travel must be established. This is done by describing lines as either Up or Down. A double track main line would be described as having Up and Down lines. If there were goods lines either side of the main lines then the four tracks could be shown as Up goods, Up main, Down main and Down goods. Sometimes the lines were in pairs, Up main Down main, Up goods, Down goods. If a modeller wishes to endow his layout with the feel of authenticity, then from the design stage onwards he should think of it as a real railway and use the correct railway terms to describe it.

It is unclear when exactly the use of the descriptions, Up and Down began. This followed existing road parlance at the start of the railway age where the Up direction led to the capital. The terms Up and Down were used on the London & Birmingham Railway at least as early as May 1839 and on the Great Western Railway from August 1840. Generally, but not always, the Down line is from London and the Up line is to London. When lines did not originate in London, other factors influenced which line would be identified as Up and Down. The advantage for modellers is that using these terms makes it easy to identify which line is which if you have specified the names of the various tracks. It is much easier for me to say, 'it is the section of the Up line between the connection at the exit of the goods branch and the Up starting signal', than to say, 'its at the left hand end of the garage, on the main line which is closest to you when you stand in the layout room, between the bridge before the start of the cassette board and where you come out of the goods sidings'. This rather garbled description is what I would have to use if I had not identified Up and Down lines on my layout. In relation to single lines, it was

The complex track formation at Newcastle Upon Tyne Central station is most often seen from above. In this 1906 view, taken at track level, it looks even more impressive, though few if any modellers would be brave enough to tackle a track layout as intricate as this.

This piece of trackwork is often referred to by modellers, as a frog. I have never been able to establish the precise origin of this expression other than to say that it is a term used in America. In British practice, the correct name for this is a common crossing. This view, taken in 1952, also shows the wing and check rails.

the direction of travel that was described as either, Up or Down.

If you use railway expressions then you are immediately closer to what you are trying to recreate in your models. Equally important is the need to correctly identify different types of points and crossings, which most modellers refer to as turnouts. In this section a variety of different track formations are illustrated and described. Looking at these is the best way to understand the structure and function of some of these aspects of permanent way construction.

Let us first define some of the terms used in connection with the permanent way.

Facing points, are those that allow traffic to move from one pair of rails to another without reversing.

Trailing points; are approached by traffic in the opposite direction to facing points.

Double junction; where two pairs of running lines diverge or converge, depending upon the direction of travel.

Tandem points; points that have two crossings and two sets of switchblades close together.

Three throw point; normally only found in goods yards, these points have their switchblades very close together and allow three possible routes to be accessed.

Scissors crossing; a trailing and facing crossover placed between a pair of running lines.

Single crossover; a trailing or facing crossover between two running lines.

Slip points; there can be be either single or double slip points. These are used in conjunction with diamond crossings. They allowed trains to be slipped between one line and the other, hence the name. However if there were no slip points, the place where two tracks cross without any connection between them would be referred to as a diamond crossing,

Crossings; the railway term for the location where two sets of running rails cross each other.

Fouling point; this term does not refer to a piece of trackwork but rather to the place where the distance between the inside rails of converging tracks is such that if a vehicle is moved closer to the point of convergence there could be a collision with a vehicle on the other track.

Connections; this is the general railway term for what modellers would usually describe as pointwork or turnouts. It is used to describe the pointwork which connects any two lines, for example, a connection between a siding and a running line or between two running lines.

To illustrate the potential complexities involved in applying the correct prototype permanent way characteristics to model trackwork, let us explore the case of the humble safety point. The application of this aspect of permanent way practice to the model railway can clearly demonstrate a modeller's understanding of the prototype, or his lack of it!

The feature in question is referred to by one of several names; throw off, safety points, catch points or trap points. These terms all describe the same thing, an arrangement for derailing trains or rolling stock in order to prevent them from coming into collision with other trains. When I was a young fireman I was somewhat confused by their various names. On asking my driver for an explanation I was told, 'trap points will derail you if you run too far forward, while catch points will put you on the floor if you run back'. This basic explanation does need to be expanded.

Trap, or as I now prefer to call them, safety points can be found at junctions between goods lines and passenger lines. They can be either single or more commonly double bladed, and may, if you run through them, put you 'on the floor' or 'off the road', to quote two railway terms. They could also be extended to form a short siding terminating at a buffer stop or stop block. This arrangement was often known as a 'blind' or 'dead end' siding. Catch points would always be placed at the start of goods loops in order to protect passenger lines directly connected to them, from any vehicle rolling back out of the loop and potentially fouling the passenger line. Similar protection was also provided in the case of connections leading from sidings and goods yards onto passenger lines.

Because they serve no purpose other than to derail trains, this feature is often omitted by modellers. Indeed, some modellers may take

exception to building something specifically for this purpose when they find many other parts of their trackwork, unintentionally, manages to do this frequently and effectively.

An alternative to safety points was a scotch block. This was a device that enabled a large block of wood to be swung across one of the running rails to prevent rolling stock from making an unauthorised movement. It was secured in place by a padlock and key, which was in the keeping of a responsible person. Though not very common, this was less expensive to install and to maintain. I have seen them modelled occasionally as an alternative to trap points. More sophisticated versions were made of iron or steel and could be lever worked from a signal box.

Trap points were also sometimes provided at the outlet of passenger bay lines at stations, though more usually the protection of the main line relied on the correct observance of the bay line signal alone. The Board of Trade for obvious reasons was not keen on the provision of facing safety points on passenger lines, other than on bay lines as described above.

The Board of Trade required runaway catch-points to be provided on gradients with an inclination steeper than 1 in 260. These points were usually held open by a spring or weight and were closed merely by the pressure of wheels passing in the proper direction, falling open again in readiness to intercept runaway vehicles, immediately the last wheels of the train had passed through. When the regulations required runaway catch points, they were usually placed at least a maximum train length for the section of line below, or to the rear of the home signal. They could also be placed below the summit and if the gradient was a long one, at intervals along the line rising to the summit.

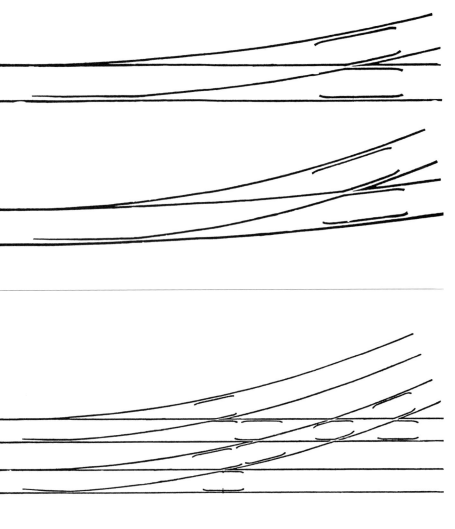

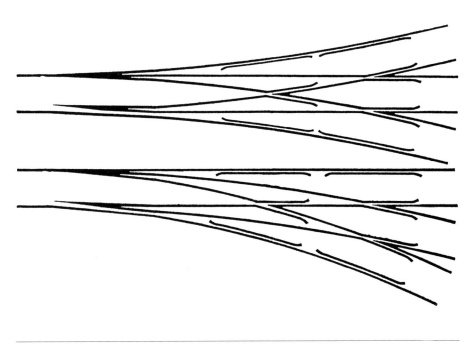

Top: **The majority of modellers use points and track that has been purchased ready made. This has both advantages and disadvantages which need to be considered. On the plus side you have points and track that can be used as soon as it has been laid and there should be no question of it not working. The disadvantage is that you will find it difficult to tailor this ready made track to suit a particular site. There is not the room here for me to discuss the practicality of track construction in detail. All I will say is that this is an option which modellers should consider. Before attempting to do this, I would recommend that you read all that you can find on the subject relating to your chosen scale.**

The drawings on this page provide examples of some of the more common connections likely to be encountered. The first drawing provides an example of facing or trailing points. The two points shown here are both left hand facing points, one is straight, the other curved. The present day description for such a piece of trackwork is a point or turnout. In years gone by these would have been described as single junctions. A point is defined as facing if the vehicles run onto it from the switchblade end and trailing if the approach is from the other end.

Centre: **This is a double junction where two lines of railway either diverge, this term is applied for a movement which is in the facing direction, or converge, where movement over the junction is in the trailing direction. Although found on goods lines, this type of connection was much more common on passenger lines**

Bottom: **Three throw points are almost always found only in goods yards. They were useful where multiple lines were required in relatively confined spaces. They are not easy to build and on the full size railways they could be troublesome. Their complexity meant that this type of pointwork could usually only be negotiated at low speeds. The diverging tracks can be on either side of a straight centre route, as in the upper drawing in our illustration, or both diverging lines could be to either the right or left hand side of the straight track. A right hand divergence is shown in the lower drawing. All of these configurations could also be built on curves.**

Above: **This picture, taken near Barton and Walton, just south of Burton on Trent, shows the main lines in the centre, with the Up and Down goods lines to either side. Note the facing connection from the main to the goods line and the way that the safety points are set so that any vehicle running back will be held by the buffer stops and not run onto the main lines. Although only part of the switchblades can be seen on the other goods line, to the right of the picture, it is clear that a similar arrangement existed on this side as well.**

Above right: **The feature illustrated in the top part of this diagram is a single trailing crossover, that below is a double crossover. Single crossovers could be laid either facing or trailing. They allow movement between two lines which are generally, but not always, parallel. A double crossover is in effect, a trailing and facing crossover laid out, one over the other. Using less space than two single crossovers, this is a very common arrangement and depending upon the way the crossover was laid out it could be either facing or trailing. The example shown here is trailing.**

Right: **This shows, above, a diamond crossing with a single slip, an arrangement that today is referred to simply as a single slip. Although diamond crossings without the switchblades are quite common, the slip arrangement in either the single or double form, shown below, is a very effective space saving track formation.**

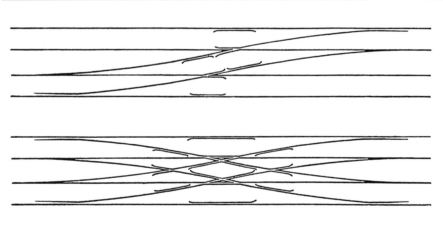

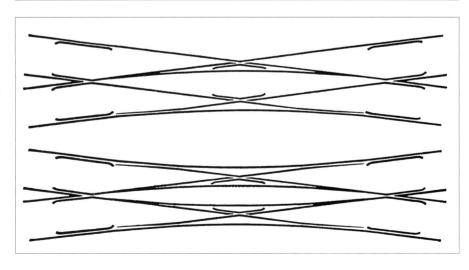

Below: **This picture, which shows part of the track layout at Bristol Temple Meads station has been included to illustrate that only by scratch building track can modellers make something like this; a scissor crossover on a slight curve, a tandem point to the right and a crossover between the platform line and centre road siding.**

Below right: **Tandem points are a bit different from the three throw points** referred to elsewhere in the book in that their switch blades are further apart. In the case of three throw points, their switch blades are grouped together. Tandem points can be arranged in a variety of ways. This one at Tewkesbury, has the centre road almost straight with the other roads diverging to the left and right. Some arrangements of tandem points are on curves, others are straight with the lines diverging, either both to the left, or to the right. W Potter

Bottom: **The connection between a colliery or an industrial line and a main line is something that is frequently modelled. This is Welbeck Colliery Branch Junction. When it is a single line, the connection should be similar to that shown here. If the connecting line was a privately owned siding, then there would normally be a gate at the point where the railway company's property ended. At this location, the facing trap point continues and becomes a short blind siding with buffer stops.**

Top right: **This picture, taken at St Albans Abbey station, provides a good detailed view of a set of safety points. The inclusion of such a piece of trackwork would add immensely to the realism of a model of a branch line terminus, such as this, though I suspect that few modellers would think to include a safety point as part of the run round arrangements. St Albans Abbey was the old L&NWR station in the city and had only a single platform face. While many locations such as this were served by push pull sets which meant that there was no need for the locomotive to run round at the terminus, there was invariably a run round loop somewhere within the layout. Here, to protect the passenger line, which was also the platform line, there were safety points at the end of the loop line and a further set on the connection to the goods siding, to the right of the picture. Here these points were controlled from the signal box which can just be seen in the distance. In other places, they could be worked from a ground frame close to where they were located.** A W V Mace Collection

Bottom right: **This example of a trap point is protecting a main line. The location is Blackwell, the station at the top of the famous Lickey incline on the outskirts of Birmingham, on the former MR line from Bristol. In this view dating from around 1960, a Jubilee class 4-6-0 is on the Down main line with an ordinary passenger train. The van to the right of the train, is standing on the short siding that leads to an end loading dock. This is a classic example of a location which needs the protection of trap points whose job is to to derail any vehicle that could move forward and foul the passenger line. The trap points are locked with the points that connect the siding to the main line, and are in effect, worked together. Only when the points are set for a movement onto the main line can the trap points be closed and the ground signal, seen in the centre right of the picture by the lamp post, be pulled off. Other details for modellers to note are the walkway alongside the siding and the short barrow crossing over the siding giving access to the platform ramp.**

Above: **I have never found any official explanation why scotch blocks were used instead of catch points. These were not the most glamourous parts of railway infrastructure and were rarely photographed. This view, taken at Evesham around 1920, is one of the best examples that I have seen. The line to the right of the siding holding the horsebox, the vehicle in the left foreground, is a transfer siding to the GWR, whose station is to the left of the picture. The connection to the right off this siding is to the Up main line. Double slip points are about half way along the side and end loading dock and to protect vehicles from fouling the main line there is a scotch block, visible just in front of the horse box. Another scotch block can also be seen, it has been swung into the clear position, and would, when placed across the rail, stop any vehicle from fouling the connection to the transfer siding and dock from the main line.**

Left: **Catch points were usually required by the Board of Trade on a line with a gradient steeper than 1 in 260. A spring or weight generally held the points open. The weight of a train passing over caused them to close. Immediately this had passed, the points opened again in readiness to catch any runaway vehicle which might have detached themselves from the train which had just passed. The points were clearly identified by a sign, sometimes this read, 'Switch', as in this instance, at other places the sign read, 'Catch Points'. The hand operated point lever behind the sign could be used to close the blades if a 'wrong road' movement was required, that would otherwise cause vehicles to be derailed. The point blades would also have to be securely clipped if a movement of this kind was to take place.**

SIGNALLING PRACTICE

The level of expertise displayed by railway modellers varies considerably, as indeed does their aims and objectives. However, I firmly believe that getting the track and signalling, right, present the greatest challenges for the modeller. Therefore I make no apologies for going into the finer points of signalling in some detail. Some may feel that I am placing too great an emphasis on signalling but if my efforts help to eliminate layouts that appear on the exhibition circuit where the signals are absent, in the wrong position or, even worse, fixed in either the on or off position, then it will be worthwhile. Apart from the appearance of the layout, operating a model railway which is correctly signalled, is very rewarding.

If you look at some of the model railways of yesteryear then signals were often conspicuous by their absence. It is not difficult to understand why this should be. Of all the elements that go to make up a model railway, signals could be considered as being the least important. Model railways will run without signals as did the full size railway in its earliest years, but most modellers are not dealing with the 1840s before signals became necessary. Today there is no excuse for lack of signalling, but there are reasons for it. One of these may be that some simply do not understand the principles of railway signalling and thus do not know what to model.

In this section I have drawn heavily upon the work of C. B. Byles, signal engineer to the Lancashire & Yorkshire Railway, whose book, *The First Principles of Railway Signalling*, was published in 1910. This is still the best book I have ever read on the development of semaphore signalling. I make no excuses for reproducing some extracts from it. At the very beginning of the book Byles asserts that, 'the operation of a railway as a commercial undertaking under the conditions existing in this country today would be absolutely impossible without a signalling system'. He defines a signalling system as, 'the whole of the means and methods whereby the movements of trains are controlled'. In my view this describes the most essential element within the operating framework for a model railway and should well be a modellers first principle.

Byles continued his introduction by saying that; 'unlike the works or the track, the signalling system of a railway is not a generic feature and, as its necessity was not completed in

the early days of railways, so it is conceivable that, with the growth of other methods, and particularly with the adoption of other means of traction, the system as we now know it maybe entirely superseded'.

Byles was not to know that nearly 100 years on, the principles of semaphore signalling he was describing would still be in evidence throughout the United Kingdom. Unlike a road vehicle, the train is confined to a track and the driver has no freedom of choice as far as his route is concerned. The only way he can avoid a collision is by stopping, while the choice of the route that he must follow lies in the hands of the signalman. The modern railway system is at its most efficient when all the trains run along a track, at the same speed, in the same direction and without conflicting movements. This was certainly not the case as far as the Victorian steam railway was concerned. Here, various classes of traffic shared the same line ranging from the fastest passenger trains that stopped only at the principal stations, to stopping freight trains that shunted every yard along the route between their starting and terminating points.

In addition to the above, there were junctions that either added more traffic or diverted some away, and seasonal peaks for both passenger, freight or mineral trains, to say nothing of special trains and adverse weather conditions. The demands of increasing traffic led to the development of the highly organised, largely mechanical, signalling system that we have to try to recreate on our models. In order to do this we need to have some understanding of how it developed, beginning with an explanation of the function of signalling.

On a railway the choice of direction does not lie with the engine driver but with the signalman. The driver can indicate, by the use of the engine whistle, the route that he wishes to follow, but only the signalman can ensure that the train travels in that direction. The first functions of a signalling system are to provide the means whereby the signalman can fulfil his responsibility for seeing that the track is clear of obstruction, and at diverging points, that the correct route is given. The other requirement of a signalling system is to communicate this information to the driver thereby establishing harmony between the train and the track.

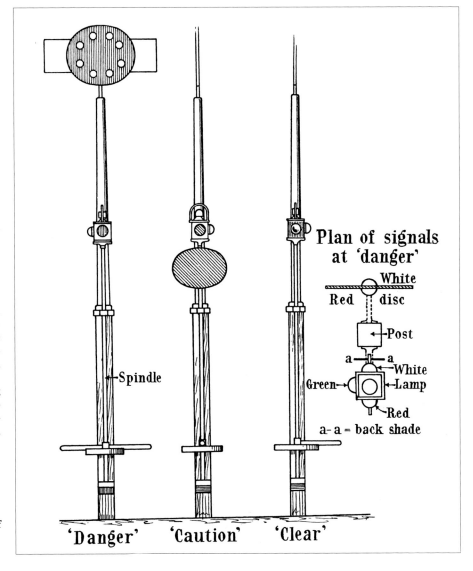

Plan of signals at 'danger'

'Danger' 'Caution' 'Clear'

The first concept of a railway was simply that it was an improved highway with rails taking the place of the road surface, on which the coaches would be drawn by engines instead of horses. These early ideas of open access did not last long. It was quickly realised that traffic had to be regulated and a method of working, evolved based upon the use of the electric telegraph and the practice of stationing men known as policemen, the forerunners of signalmen, at intervals along the line. Between the 1840s and the end of the century a system of signalling evolved from those primitive beginnings that was to outlast steam traction on BR.

The first idea of train control was that by keeping a good time interval between trains there would be little chance of one overtaking another. At the few junctions and crossing points trains would wait their turn, or as an alternative, every train would come to a stand before reaching the junction. Soon it was found necessary to station men, who were known as policemen, at places where trains might be stopped. They were to be found at stations and junctions and they were expected to signal drivers to stop if circumstances made it necessary for them to do so. The idea was that the line should be clear as a matter of course when the train arrived and if the policemen were not to be seen, the driver assumed that such was the case.

At first the policemen used hand or flag signals. These were soon supported by the provision of the first fixed signals. These enabled the policeman to exhibit a danger signal and leave it exhibited when he himself was not present. The fixed signal was at first only regarded as a substitute for the policeman. However these ideas were soon to change as traffic levels greatly increased.

Byles noted four phases in the development of the British railway signalling systems. It was found that at certain places it was necessary to provide fixed signals to take the place of the hand signals exhibited by policemen. Thus the first stage in the traffic requirements was the need to provide the means of providing a signal to drivers to stop.

As traffic levels and the speed of trains increased, it became even more essential that trains should stop when and where required to do so. The siting of station signals was such that sometimes they could not always be seen by drivers in time to stop, In these cases the need for an additional signal, to the rear of the stop signal became necessary. These signals, known at first as auxiliary signals, soon came to be called distant signals. Their use was at first restricted to places where cuttings, tunnels or other local conditions, made it difficult for the driver to see the stop signal in time to stop. The provision of these signals, marked the second stage of the development of signalling.

The further increase in the number of trains and the fact that their speeds were beginning to vary, brought other problems. Whereas it was necessary to provide protection within the station limits, it now became necessary to protect trains while they were between stations, to prevent faster trains from overtaking slower ones. To overcome this problem the time interval system was devised. The policemen at the various signalling stations would exhibit their danger signals immediately a train had passed them. The danger signal would continue to be exhibited for a given time, usually five minutes, and until that time had elapsed, no train was allowed to follow. For a further period of time a caution signal would be shown, or the driver of the following train would be stopped and told what sort of train was in front of him, and how long ago it had passed. Having received this caution, he would be allowed to proceed. After the expiry of a further period of time the all-right signal would be shown and a following train would be allowed to pass unchecked.

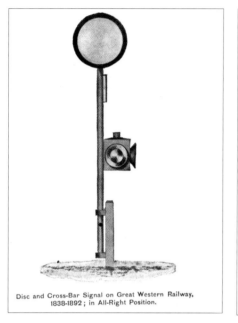

Disc and Cross-Bar Signal on Great Western Railway, 1838-1892; in All-Right Position.

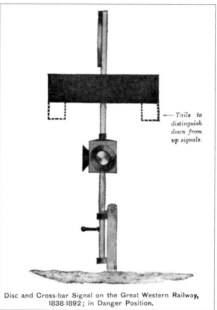

←— Tails to distinguish down from up signals.

Disc and Cross-bar Signal on the Great Western Railway, 1838-1892; in Danger Position.

Not every block post was a signal box. Some were inside station buildings and in this instance, on the station platform, exposed to the elements. This picture was taken in 1927 at Bethesda in North Wales, the terminus of the short ex-LNWR branch from Bangor. In addition to the point and signal levers, the level crossing gates were also controlled from here. The signal diagram and the telegraphic instrument in the box are both mounted onto the paled fence. G H Platt

The time interval system was better than nothing and while it was practicable for regulating light traffic, as traffic levels increased, it became cumbersome. In order to make provision for contingencies a longer time interval had to be maintained than was necessary to enable the train in front to get sufficiently ahead. The time interval system was the third stage of the development of signalling systems identified by Byles .

The idea of a space or block interval system worked by means of electrical apparatus originated around 1850. It became known as the block system. Early installations were at tunnels such as that at Clay Cross in Derbyshire, and on steep gradients. The use of this system was gradually extended and by the 1870s the block system had become established on the main lines of the leading railway companies. It was not, however, until after the passing of the Regulation of Railways Act of 1889 that block working was made obligatory for all passenger carrying lines in Great Britain and Ireland. This Act established the principles on which British railway signalling was to be based until well into the next century.

The gradual developments described above were accompanied by a corresponding evolution in the equipment employed to signal trains. At first each company did its own thing as is evidenced by the disc signal used by the London & Birmingham Railway illustrated earlier on page 27. This was quite different to the disc and crossbar type used on the Great Western and illustrated on the page opposite. In time a degree of uniformity was established between the signalling equipment used by the different companies.

The traditional semaphore signal had its origins in a form of signalling used for military and naval purposes. Before the invention of the electric telegraph, which totally transformed the other methods of sending messages over long distances, the naval and military authorities used a system of telegraphs worked by means of moveable arms on posts. They were fixed on adjacent hilltops and by a combination of movements, messages were sent over long distances, providing those on the next hilltop could see the signals from the previous one. These were known as semaphore telegraphs. The word semaphore, according to *The First Principles of Railway Signalling,* means, 'that which bears a sign'. Around 1840 the semaphore was first applied to railway signalling and by the 1860s it was in general use on Britain's railway system.

Early signals were worked by means of a handle on the signal post and the policemen in charge had to run from signal to signal in order to operate them. In due course the idea evolved that the various levers working the signals should be concentrated at a convenient spot. The points however still continued to be worked by levers fixed close to them and there was generally no connection between the points and signals. This led to accidents due to either points or signals being incorrectly set or set for conflicting movements. The next step therefore, was to bring both the signal and point levers to one place and then interlock them so that no contradictory movements could be made. The first locking frame, using this principle, was erected at Bricklayers Arms in London in 1856 followed in 1861 by one at Stratford, also in London.

As far as railway modellers today are concerned, few layouts have full interlocking of points and signals. The modeller uses arrangements superseded on the prototype by around 1870!

Broadly speaking signalling must protect the train from obstructions and provide an indication of the direction of travel. The obstructions that trains could encounter were points and crossings not set for their direction of travel, stationary vehicles on the same track ahead of the train or moving along tracks that crossed over the one that the train was travelling along. The most frequently encountered danger of obstruction was caused by a train travelling on the same line. The danger of a collision from the rear was a very real one.

In addition to protecting trains from obstructions the signalling system must also provide the indication of direction. Therefore at points of divergence there must be signals which, by their form and grouping, indicate the direction which the train is to follow and to some extent, the nature of the route. However, before looking at different types of signals let us define some of the more common terms associated with signalling.

The commonest signalling term of all is probably the signal box itself. It was originally called a section post, but later came to be described as a block post, a term which linked it to the block system. Usually, but not always, a block post was a signal box manned by a signalman. At some locations, usually stations on branch lines, there was not a signal box as such, the block instruments being kept in the station building with the station master rather than a signalman in charge of them. In some instances (see opposite), the levers could be in the open on the platform.

The signal box controlled a block section. This was the length of track between adjacent block posts, into which only one train was usually permitted to enter at a time. The immediate area around the signal box, if it was at a station was known as the station limits. This was sometimes referred to as the yard. It was the area between the home signal (or outer home if one existed) and the most advanced starting signal. The signal box had to be located in a position where the signalman had a view of the whole of the running lines comprising his yard.

Trains were controlled by a variety of fixed signals. These varied in details of their design from company to company. In Britain fixed signals were generally of three distinct types. When at danger, the signal arm in all cases assumed a horizontal position. Upper quadrant signals were raised to show a clear aspect, lower quadrant signals pointed in the other direction, downwards, to do this. Somersault signals pivoted in the centre of the signal arm, their all right aspect had the arm parallel with the signal post. There were two main types of fixed signals conveying one of two messages to the driver. A stop signal could indicate all right or danger, distant signals all right or caution. The danger indication on stop signals was always shown except when the signalman had given permission for a train movement to take place. Trains could pass distant signals when they displayed the caution indication. The purpose of distants was to show the position of the road ahead. If a distant signal was on, it meant that the next stop signal was at danger.

Therefore, in so far as through running was concerned, distant signals were the most important of the main line signals, as they gave the key to the situation ahead of the train. Distant signals were distinguished by having a V shaped notch cut into the end of the signal arm. For obvious reasons this was sometimes referred to as a fishtail. When a distant signal was at caution it indicated that some or all of the stop signals ahead, controlled by the signal box whose distant signal this was, were at danger. When it displayed the all right or clear signal, that indicated that those stop signals mentioned above, were also showing clear. A distant signal is the first indication to a driver has that he may have to stop at the next home signal and that it had to be sufficiently far back from the home signal to enable him to do so. This distance varied according to gradients and other circumstances.

Where there were short block sections other arrangements had to be made. A distant signal could be placed below either the home or starting signal for the box in the rear. Sometimes, when the block section was very short, a distant arm was placed below both the home and starting signal. These were known as the inner and outer distant signals.

Although distant signals were intended to show the position of all stop signals in advance, there were some locations where a fixed distant signal was used. This was fixed to the post and could not be pulled off. These were used in advance of locations where there was a permanent requirement to slow down or stop and acted as reminder of this to drivers.

For many years the arms of distant signals were painted the same colour as stop signals, namely red. They showed a red light at night when at caution and green when pulled off. In the first decades of the twentieth century, there was concern that drivers were sometimes confused with potentially fatal results by the fact that both home and distant signals were the same colour. Shortly after grouping it was decided that the arms of distant signals were to be painted yellow and that they were to display a yellow light at night when at caution. By this time the Irish Free State had seceded from the United Kingdom so the new regime did not apply there. Though the yellow and green aspects at night were adopted, to this day, sem-

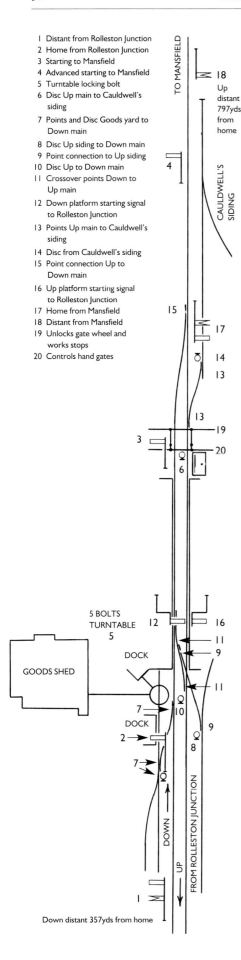

1 Distant from Rolleston Junction
2 Home from Rolleston Junction
3 Starting to Mansfield
4 Advanced starting to Mansfield
5 Turntable locking bolt
6 Disc Up main to Cauldwell's siding
7 Points and Disc Goods yard to Down main
8 Disc Up siding to Down main
9 Point connection to Up siding
10 Disc Up to Down main
11 Crossover points Down to Up main
12 Down platform starting signal to Rolleston Junction
13 Points Up main to Cauldwell's siding
14 Disc from Cauldwell's siding
15 Point connection Up to Down main
16 Up platform starting signal to Rolleston Junction
17 Home from Mansfield
18 Distant from Mansfield
19 Unlocks gate wheel and works stops
20 Controls hand gates

Southwell station

Left: This drawing of Southwell station shows the layout at a station on a single line with a long passing loop. Passenger trains terminated here before returning to Rolleston Junction from the same platform. The track formation was altered in 1929 and further details about Southwell will be found in *LMS Journal: Preview Issue.* **This drawing is based upon an original Midland Railway one found at the Public Record Office, Kew. It is included here for several reasons; the first being that a passing loop through a station is a popular track layout with many modellers. The plan also provides evidence that it is not necessary to move the coaches to another platform before the return journey is made and also shows why an advanced starting signal is necessary. At Southwell any engine running round a train in the platform would have to go into the section beyond the starting signal towards Mansfield, but the presence of an advanced starting signal means that all movements are within station limits. On the original plan the points were not numbered but fortunately a plan dated 1903, in the Dunbar Collection, contains this information. This diagram also confirms that signal box lever 5 bolted the wagon turntable. With 5 reversed and point 7 and home signal 2 locked in the normal position, a collision was prevented if a wagon was being turned on the wagon turntable. Finally ground disc 7 works with points 7, acting as a point indicator.**
Drawing and notes, A E Overton

Right: This drawing, based on an example shown in *The First Principles of Railway Signalling,* **illustrates signalling arrangements on a double line with a loop, where the sections were short. As was discussed on the previous page, in many instances, the posts carrying the home signals for one signal box would also carry a distant operated by the box ahead. Where two ground signals are together, for example on this drawing beside signal box B, the normal signalling practice was for the top signal to read to the left, and the bottom one to read to the right.**
Drawing A E Overton

Down distant for B (controlled as outer distant for A)

Up starter for B

Down inner distant for A
Down home for 13
Signal box B works signals that are unshaded

Up home for B

UP
DOWN

Up inner home/starting signal for A
Up inner distant for B
Down home for A

Signal box A works signals that are shaded

Up outer home for A
Up outer distant for B

Down starter for A

Ground signals.

Where there are two ground signals the top arm reads to the left, bottom to the right

Up outer distant for A

aphore distant signals in what is now the Irish Republic, continue to be painted red.

Before we leave the subject of distant signals, from my own experience on the railway, I can vouch for their importance. As a fireman, spotting the state of the distant signal at the earliest moment for my driver was most important. If it was all right, we could relax, knowing the road was clear. At Saltley we called them, 'backuns', and although I have never seen the word written down I suspect it came from the fact that, when they were introduced, the distant signal was described as being, 'back one from the home signal'.

The home signal protects the first occurring obstruction, whether it is a siding, junction points or crossover. A highway level crossing, being movable, was not always classed as an obstruction. Some sources suggest that a passenger platform is an obstruction, a view that I share, and it must be protected by a signal. The home signal must be placed before the fouling point of the obstruction. It is usual to allow a margin between the home signal and the actual fouling point. If the signal box was provided to create a block section only and there were no connections or other forms of local obstructions to be protected, the home signal would usually be placed as near the signal box as possible. This was to enable the signalman to communicate with a driver who might be held at that signal. Where there were no connections or potential obstructions to protect, the home signal was also the starting signal. In such a place, there was no necessity to provide separate starting signal. However one is usually provided to enable a train waiting to proceed to be brought within the protection of the home signal that would be to the rear of the train. It is essential that a train brought to a stand at a home signal should be well within the view of the signal box, or failing this, apparatus to indicate to the signalman the presence of the train, should be provided.

In cases where the points worked from a signal box were numerous and were spread out over a considerable length of main line, it was often necessary to provide one or more inner home signals ahead of the home signal itself. The necessity for and the placing of inner home signals was determined by local circumstances.

The trackplan of Southwell in Nottinghamshire, on page 30, illustrates the circumstances where an advanced starting signal is required. A train on the Down line could be held at signal 3 while a train approached from the other direction. When signal 3 was pulled off, the Down train was still within station limits until it passed signal 4, the advanced starting signal, and entered the block section. This meant that if there was a requirement to move a train, or in this instance, if the locomotive of a working terminating at the Down platform was required to run round stock, then it was possible to move beyond the starting signal out as far as the advanced starting signal and still be within station limits. In a location where there was no advanced starting signal, any movement in advance of the starting signal would require the train to be offered to the signalman in advance because it would be entering the next block section.

The lowering or clearing of a signal arm (other than that of a distant signal) gives permission to proceed up to the next signal whether at that particular signal box or at the signal box in advance. However, it was sometimes necessary, usually at large stations, to bring a train past a signal while the line, between that signal and the next one was occupied. This frequently happened at terminal stations and sometimes also at junctions where trains had to be remarshalled. One way of doing this was to stop the train at the signal box by a flag signal and inform the driver of the state of things ahead. Without this verbal

warning, he could not have been expected to be prepared to stop clear of any obstruction.

The drawbacks with this method of working can be imagined. At busy places it was far from convenient and was liable to lead to mistakes. To avoid this possibility, a type of signal known as a calling on arm, was introduced. These small semaphore arms were often placed under home signals on the same post. The lowering of a calling on signal conveyed to the driver the information that would otherwise have had to be given verbally, namely that he could pass the main signal at danger but that he had to proceed with caution and be prepared to stop as the line between the calling on arm and the next stop signal, was blocked.

To ensure that the driver had his train well under control it was usual to insist that the train must come to a stand before a calling on arm was lowered. These arms often showed no light when at danger and a small green light when lowered. Generally when the home signal was lowered the calling-on arm remained at danger. At some locations, where no calling on arm was provided, the clearing of the main signal arm after the train was at or nearly at a stand, gave the same message to the driver as a calling arm would have done.

Related to calling on signals were siding and shunting signals. Both the design and employment of these signals varied from company to company. When a shunting movement on a main line or through points worked from a signal box was not governed by a fixed signal, the signalman had to give a hand signal from the box. Hand signals were liable to be misunderstood, particularly if more than one engine happened to be in the neighbourhood and if the shunting movements were frequent. In such places shunt signals were common. On the other hand, at a roadside station where little shunting took place, these operations would often be controlled by hand signals.

This photograph shows one of the most common of junction layouts, that between a single line and a double line. Broom was one of my favourite railway locations, where the single line of the erstwhile Stratford on Avon & Midland Junction Railway, from Stratford, joined the Midland line from Barnt Green to Ashchurch, between Redditch and Evesham. The junction at Broom was what I would call a, Victorian junction, meaning that it was over engineered by later standards in relation to the amount of traffic which it had to handle. A simpler layout would probably have sufficed but when the line was built, this was not permitted. This picture, taken from the road bridge, shows the line to Stratford to the left and the single line to Evesham straight ahead. The wagons in the distance are on two sidings, with a line leading to a turntable to the right.

Therefore the extent to which shunting and siding signals were provided depended upon the circumstances.

It was usual to provide a signal at the points leading from a siding to a main line and usually at the points of a crossover. Signals were frequently provided also for setting back from a main line to a siding, Some companies went further and provided a shunting signal for every possible shunting movement on main lines and also within sidings, so far as the movements were made over points worked from a signal box. Of the 'Big Four' companies which were created in 1924, the Great Western Railway was undoubtedly the most generous when it came to the provision of signals to cover shunting movements. The variety of types of siding and shunting signals employed was very great. They could be either low semaphores with small arms and lights, semaphores standing some two or three feet above rail level, revolving lamps or circular discs. These signals either protected obstructions or indicated the direction on similar principles to those relating to running signals.

So far we have only discussed semaphore signals, but it must be remembered that colour light signals were in use in Britain throughout the last century. Railway writers in the 1920s and earlier referred to these as, 'daylight colour signals'. The earlier examples were single aspect signals which consisted of special electric lamps and lenses, hooded to enable them to be seen by drivers from distance in daylight. The colours displayed by these signals were the same as those given by semaphores at night, red or green for the stop signals or yellow and green for distants.

A common use of colour light signals was as intermediate block signals. Some references describe colour light signals as 'IB' signals, which is misleading. There were, and still are, semaphore intermediate block signals in service. These signals, both colour light and semaphore, were used to shorten block sections and thereby increase the line occupancy, without having to build extra signal boxes. In some places the installation of intermediate block signals enabled the railway companies to close a signal box whose only function was to

The Halesowen branch, to the south west of Birmingham, was a joint GW and LMS line where the LMS rule book applied. Rubery was the only passing place on this short branch line that was worked on the electric token block system using a staff rather than a token. The staffs used on the branch were colour coded. Between Halesowen and Rubery they were blue and between Rubery and Longbridge West, where the branch joined the former MR main line to Bristol, the colour was green. This picture is a little unusual in that it would not be normal practice for all three members of the crew of the goods, driver, fireman and guard, to stand on the platform to watch a train go by, but this was a rare passenger working on the branch in the form of an enthusiasts' special. The signalman is standing in the 'six foot' waiting to exchange staffs with the driver of the special. P B Whitehouse

shorten a block section. Colour light signals were more economical to maintain than conventional semaphore signals and the emphasis from 1923 onwards was to achieve greater economy of working. When intermediate block signals were installed, the signal box in the rear normally controlled them.

In the early decades of the railway network in Britain, signals were usually located very close to the signal box which controlled them. Up to the around the 1870s, it was usual to find junction signals placed immediately over the signal box, rather than at the actual point of obstruction. A driver finding his signal at danger would not be entitled to run up to the signal, as became the later practice, he would have to ensure that he stopped well clear of the junction itself.

From the 1880s onwards at junctions between converging lines, a home signal had now to be provided in each direction. Its position was determined by the first occurring fouling point, which was either the fouling point of the converging route or that of some connection or other form of obstruction short of the junction itself. In the diverging or facing direction, the junction home signals, in like manner, protected the first occurring obstruction. If the first point to be protected was the junction points themselves, the home signal would be placed clear of the locking bar, so that a train standing at the signal could not be brought to a stand on the bar. These signals not only protected the points but they also had to indicate the direction in which the points were set. For this purpose a separate arm was be provided for each direction, the arms being placed side by side in the order in which the respective routes diverged. It was usual to indicate the relative importance of the routes by making the arm for the more important route the highest. An older method was to place two or even three signal arms, one over the other, on a single post. This was superseded by the system of having a post for each route, the lowest post being for the least important route. This was called, stepping the arms, and a junction signal applying to several routes could have arms on posts of three or four different heights.

In the exceptional case of a main line junction leading in one direction to a siding or dead end, the arm for this direction was to be a smaller one than the others, and showed smaller lights by night. Signals protecting junctions in the facing direction were usually fixed on bracket posts and are referred to as bracket signals. If there were more signal arms required than could be accommodated on brackets, or if space for a bracket post in the proper position was not available, the arms were mounted upon a signal bridge. Today this structure is usually described as a signal gantry

One theme running through the development of signalling over the decades is an increasing level of technological sophistication in signalling practice. Starting with a man with a flag, about as basic as it can get, signals were then grouped together under one roof. The telegraph is introduced to determine the whereabouts of trains along the line. Then the rudiments of interlocking between signals and points were introduced to prevent signalmen setting up conflicting movements. Another major advance came in the early years of the last century when power signalling was introduced. The difference between a manual and a power installation was that in a manual box the power required to pull the levers to manipulate the signals and points was supplied by the physical exertions of the signalman. In a power installation, this force was derived from an outside source such as electricity or compressed air and very little physical effort was needed on the part of the signalman. It was also argued that signalman was less fatigued if he was spared the physical effort of pulling heavy levers all day. In turn this made him more alert mentally and less likely to be the cause of an incident through a loss of concentration caused by tiredness.

Power signalling also paved the way for semi-automatic signals. Operated by either the train or the signalman, these could be either colour lights or semaphores. Semi-automatic signals were used as intermediate block signals to break up long block sections. They could also be used to allow access to sidings, perhaps via a ground frame released by the signalman. They would normally function automatically, activated by the passage of trains. As required, however, the signalman could intervene and take control of the signal to allow a route to be changed or a siding to be entered.

The final step in the evolution of signalling to date has been the installation of automatic signalling. Here the working of the signals is controlled automatically by the movements of the trains themselves. The passage of a train along a stretch of line turns the signals it passes to danger until it has progressed to the point where the signals in its rear are automatically cleared for the passage of following trains. The trains and the signals in a sense, create their own block into which no other working can pass until it is safe to do so. Whilst signalling now had reached great heights of technical progress using state of the art electronics and all kinds of sophisticated computer controls, the basic idea, that of allowing only one train to occupy a defined stretch of line at a time, goes back to the very dawn of the railway age, for that was also the aspiration of those policemen with their flags.

So far we have mostly focused on the signalling of double track routes but of course in Great Britain there was a considerable mileage of single line railway on which traffic had to be worked safely. We touched on this subject in relation to the layout at Southwell (see page 30), where a double track line became single beyond the station. Single line railways have always been very popular with modellers, so how are they worked and what challenges do they present for those who wish to replicate their operation authentically?

On the prototype, safe operation was achieved by maintaining a space interval longitudinally in respect of following movements and laterally in respect of converging and crossing movements, exactly as on double lines. In other words single lines were worked by a variant of the block system.

Prior to the passing of the Railway Regulation Act of 1889, the crossing order system, widely used overseas, in particular in the USA, was used on many single lines in this country. Under this system, when it became necessary for trains to cross one another at a place other than that laid down for them in the working timetable, telegraphic instructions were sent from some central office. Receipt of such instructions by the trainmen and station staffs provided the necessary authority for the regular crossing place to be changed.

The Railway Regulation Act of 1889 gave the Board of Trade power to order the adoption of the block system generally and it included in the orders a requirement that single lines should be worked on one of three methods: the train staff, train staff and ticket or the electric staff or tablet. Each of these systems was based upon the principle that the same object could not be in two places at once and that the possession of that object was the sole authority for a driver to enter the section of single line to which it applied. The rules of each of these systems were designed to ensure that not more than one train could be on the same stretch of single line at the same time. The train staff and the electric staff or tablet systems provide security against trains overtaking as well as against their meeting head on, the train staff and ticket system did not guard against overtaking and had to be supplemented by the block telegraph.

The train staff system was mainly used for working lengths of single line over which a train worked backwards and forwards between a junction and branch terminus. The usual arrangement was for a wooden staff, about two foot long and lettered with the name of the section, to be provided. Possession of this staff was the sole authority for a driver to proceed along the single line. It follows that only one engine driver could have the staff at any one time. Two engines coupled together were allowed onto the line provided that they remained coupled for the duration of their stay.

In most cases, apart from short branch lines, it was likely that a situation could arise where more than one train was required to pass over the single line section in the same direction consecutively. A train staff alone was not suitable for this contingency because it was necessary to return the staff from the other end before the second train could travel over the line. One method of overcoming this problem was to use the staff and ticket system. At the staff stations at either end of a section, a supply of specially printed coloured tickets was provided and were kept in a box locked with a spring lock. This box could only be opened by a key attached to or forming part of the staff. If more than one train had to pass through the section in the same direction before a train was to pass in the opposite direction, the driver of each such train, except the last, was merely shown the staff and was given a ticket. This was his authority to travel through the section on the strength of having seen the staff. The tickets gave authority for a movement in one direction only and were, therefore of no use for an opposite movement. The last train of the series took the staff and when it was given up to the signalman at the other end of the section, it could then be used to allow movements in the opposite direction. As at the other end of the section, the key either attached to, or forming the end of the staff, could be used to unlock the ticket box to authorise multiple movements in that direction.

This system was not ideal for working lines where the traffic was irregular. Should the staff be at the wrong end of the single line section, then a train would have to be held until it was returned by messenger. When a train had entered the section with a ticket, there was nothing, so far as the staff system working was concerned, to prevent another train from following with another ticket or the staff. Therefore, in order to maintain the space interval for following trains, ordinary block working had to be established. Block indicators were used in the middle of a block section to remind signalmen of the direction in which the trains were moving and to prevent them from initiating a conflicting movement.

In principle the electric train staff and tablet systems were identical. The tablet was a metal disc generally about six inches in diameter, and the electric train staff was made of metal, about the same size as an ordinary staff that was made of wood. The tablets were placed in a leather pouch before being handed to the drivers. The pouch was attached to a hoop shaped handle, which enabled tablets to be exchanged between the signalman and the fireman while the train was moving. Then the hoop, with the tablet in the pouch was hung onto a hook in the engine cab until the next exchange point. Other variants of this system involved miniature electric staffs about six inches long and key tokens.

I got a thorough grounding in this method of working when I spent a year in the Evesham link at Saltley shed in Birmingham. The northern section of this line from Barnt Green to Evesham was single line with passing loops. In my book, *An Illustrated History of the Ashchurch To Barnt Green Line, the Evesham Route,* (Oxford Publishing Company, 2002), I have reproduced the signalling diagrams for each of the stations. Readers wishing to learn more about single line working may find this book helpful.

The electric staff, like the ordinary train staff mentioned earlier, carried the name of the section to which it applied. The staffs and their associated equipment were usually, though not exclusively, kept in signal boxes. As staff or

tablet stations were places where trains would converge in order to cross, they had to be fully signalled. The signals were similar to those used on an ordinary double line.

The conditions under which trains were allowed to approach a block or staff post on a single line were the same as those applying on double lines, with one exception. In order to cross each other two trains had to approach a passing loop at a staff station from opposite directions, often for traffic purposes so as not to cause delays, virtually simultaneously. They were much closer together than they would have been on a conventional double track layout. Trains were therefore allowed to approach provided the line was clear up to the signal at the end of the loop line into which they had to run. The signals at the entrance to the loop were kept at danger. The train arriving first was admitted and when it had come to a stand in the loop line and it was clear to the signalman that it was not fouling the other line, the train from the opposite direction was allowed to enter.

Junctions between single lines or between a double line and a single line were usually formed as a double line junction and the ordinary signalling arrangements applied both in respect of block working and in the arrangement of the outdoor signals. The layout at Broom North, pictured on page 31, is a good example of this.

In some circumstances, for traffic reasons, a siding was required in the middle of a single track section where there was no signal box. Access to such sidings was usually controlled by a ground frame or, as it was referred to by the Midland Railway, a stage. The normal method of unlocking the ground frame was by means of a key on the train staff for that section. This meant that only the crew of a train with the proper authority to be in that section could enter the siding. No other traffic could pass along the single line section whilst the staff or token was in their possession.

Therefore a train shunting at such a siding that was in the section was perfectly safe and no signals were required to protect the shunting operation. However, the points leading to the siding would always be facing in one direction and the safety points, which protected the main lines from any vehicles that might be pushed along the siding onto the main line, had to be secured. Locking the lever that worked these points, by means of a key that formed part of the train staff, provided the security that was required. The key could not be removed from the lever frame unless the points were returned to their normal position, that is, set for the main line. Until that key was handed over at the end of the section, another train could not go onto the single line.

This principle also applied if the line was worked using tablets or tokens instead of train staffs. In that case the tablet was placed in a slide in the lever frame and acted as a key to unlock the frame so that the levers could be moved. While the shunting was taking place

the staff or tablet could not be withdrawn until the points had been returned to their normal position.

The placement of a siding on a section of single track was a potential hazard to other traffic unless, as we have seen, access to it was carefully and safely managed by the line's signalling equipment. Although most modellers appear to want their railway to be perfectly flat, gradients exist on the real thing. The question of runaway catch points on double lines has already been discussed. Severe gradients and the possibility of runaways also exist on single lines, however, it will be realised that on single lines an open catch point in one direction becomes a trap point in the other and this would derail traffic which had every right to be there travelling in that direction. If a crossing loop occurred on a gradient the risk of vehicles within the loop running back onto the single line was prevented by providing a catch point worked from the signal box, just clear of the converging point of the two loops. As the risk of breakaway was always the greatest where trains had to be brought to a stand, the Board of Trade did not allow a station or a siding connection on a single line where the gradient was steeper than 1 in 260, unless certain precautions were taken.

If it was necessary to provide a station on such a gradient, it had to be a double line station, with catch points being provided at the lower end of the loop as explained above. In the case of a siding connection on a gradient, there must either be a loop, as in the case of a station, in order that a train having to call at the siding may be left standing on the loop and within the catch point when the engine is detached. Failing that, one of two other methods had to be adopted. There must be sufficient room inside the sidings for the whole train to be placed there, clear of the main line, before the engine was detached for shunting operations. Alternatively, the railway company had to undertake to have an engine at the lower end of trains calling at the siding. Such an arrangement would be very inconvenient to say the least, nevertheless such undertakings, given under the company's seal, were required by the Board of Trade for these operations to be sanctioned.

In the nineteenth century both the railway companies and the Board of Trade were very conscious of the potential hazards of facing points. Whilst I doubt if many layout builders will wish to produce working examples of facing point locks on their models, unless in a large scale, as they can be replicated, I will make a brief reference to them. Facing point locks were introduced, as far back as the 1870s and were intended to prevent several causes of accidents. One such instance occurred when the switch blades of points remained partly open when the lever working the points was pulled. If the switchblades were not firmly home against the stock rail, a train passing over them would be derailed. A point lock prevented this happening. Locks also meant that

A method of working branch lines, used by many British railway companies, was the motor train, auto train or pull and push set, to give several of the names applied to these vehicles. The principle was the same, the locomotive stayed at one end of the coaches all the time. When pulling the stock, the driver and fireman shared the cab in the usual way, but when the loco was pushing the stock, the driver occupied a driving position in the leading coach. This LMS set is working on the Delph branch in Lancashire. Here the driver receives the token for the single line section ahead from the signalman.

Above left: **Here we can see the fireman of BR Standard Class 5 4-6-0 No 73001, on a Bournemouth to Bristol passenger train, about to pick up the tablet at Midford, on the former Somerset & Dorset line, for the single line section to Bath Junction. The tablet is contained in a leather pouch, which is attached to the loop. Many signal boxes where tablet exchanges took place had platforms similar to the one seen here. The arrangement of the steps to enable the signalman to be at the right height to make the exchange and guard rail to prevent him from falling were commonplace at places where tablets were exchanged.**
Paul Cotterell

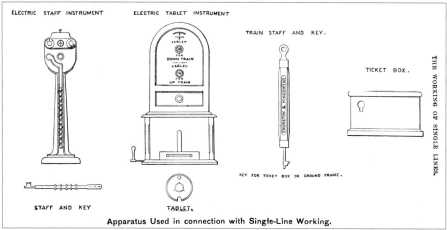

Apparatus Used in connection with Single-Line Working.

Below left: **This drawing shows some of the pieces of apparatus which were used in connection with single line working. The electric staff instrument, on the far left, held the staffs, one of which is illustrated below. When this was withdrawn from the instrument and handed to the driver, it was his authority to travel through the single line section. The key on the end of the staff could be used to open a ground frame in the section, as described in the text. The electric tablet system worked on the same principle as the electric staff, tablets were kept in the instrument until released. The key on the end of the train staff, third from left, was used to open the ticket box, which is also illustrated, if a line was being worked on the staff and ticket system.**

points could be not be moved while a train was passing over them.

The systems used by companies to lock their facing points varied. Some, notably the Midland, worked the facing point lock and the points by the same lever, while one company inserted a wedge between the switch and the stock rail in place of providing a blade and plunger. The drawing opposite on page 37, shows the arrangement where there is a separate lever for the point switchblades and another for the facing point lock. In this example, the signals were also locked electrically.

Another problem which was a cause of accidents over the years arose when the fouling point between converging tracks could not be clearly seen from the signal box. In that situation, there was the risk that the signalman might inadvertently give permission for a movement that could lead to a collision. To overcome this problem fouling, or as they were also known, locking bars, were fitted. They were similar to the facing point locks and came in various designs and lengths. However the principle was the same, if a vehicle's wheels

were on the fouling bar, the signalman was prevented from moving those points.

Perhaps the greatest contribution to the evolution of a safer railway came with the concept of interlocking. The interlocking of points and signals prevented conflicting movements being signalled. In mechanical signal boxes the signals and points were worked from the box by means of levers grouped together in the interlocking frame. The movement of the levers was transmitted to the points by means of rods and to the signals by wires. At one time points were also worked by a single weighted wire. Although this method of actuating points by wire generally ceased well before the grouping on lines open for passenger traffic, a few examples survived in goods yards until much later.

The levers in the frame were interlocked in such a manner that it was impossible for an unsafe combination of lever movements to be made. For example, a lever working a mainline signal could not be moved unless the levers working the points on the route to which it applied, were in their proper position

and, if there were facing points, until these were properly secured by the facing point locks. This meant that some levers were in the normal or forward position and others in the reverse position when in the frame. There were a number of different ways by which interlocking was achieved and the subject is worth further study by those interested in the subject. As a starting point, a drawing of a locking frame is shown on page 39.

Most modellers, and until recently I was not an exception, do not fully interlock their points and signals. The problem on a large complex layout is that errors happen, but if you have a fully interlocked system then you should be error free. Operator error is the usual reason for a derailment or similar mistake on a layout at an exhibition, I know, I have often been responsible for them when I have been operating. However, I have operated layouts that have fully interlocked lever frames and as a result I can say that, in my view, nothing provides greater operating realism. There is great satisfaction in moving the levers in the correct order and seeing the points change and the signals move. The problem for most modellers is understanding the principles which governed the sequence for interlocking the points and signals. After reading reports that were made by the inspecting officers of the Board of Trade, it is clear that the interlocking installed by some railway companies did not always meet with the inspectors' approval. The inspector's test was to try to move the levers to see if he could set up a conflicting movement. If he was able to do this, he would want changes to be made to the locking arrangements before sanctioning the use of the installation for traffic.

The subject of interlocking is complex, which is why most modellers do not attempt to install it on their layouts. When Dewsbury was exhibited, a major problem we encountered was one which was usually described as, operator error. What used to happen with Dewsbury was that, because the controls were not interlocked, the operator sometimes forgot to reverse a section switch or to return points to normal. If this happened, things could go wrong, not often but enough to convince me that I had to alter the method of working. It was therefore decided that the layout had to be rebuilt with a fully interlocked control system. This work will make the it much more realistic in operating terms.

The key to successful interlocking is to set the points before the signals. Therefore if a train was to travel over a facing junction the locking arrangements would only permit the signal levers to be pulled after the points had been set. After the point lever has been pulled, the signals would be cleared in the sequence, home, starting and finally distant signal. When the train had passed, the sequence of returning the signal levers to normal would be in reverse order, and finally the point levers would be put back. A basic test to see whether interlocking is working or not is that it should not be possible to pull the signals off unless the points are set for the direction of travel indicated by the signals.

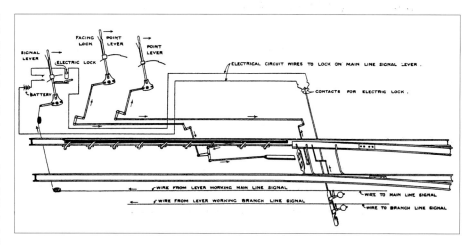

Top right: **This drawing demonstrates some of the equipment required for facing points including a facing point lock and bar and mechanical detectors. This arrangement required two levers, one for the lock and the other for the point lever. It was possible to work both with one lever. This was a method favoured by the Midland Railway.**

Right: **This is a most interesting location. The view is of Canal Bridge signal box on the Gloucester New Docks branch. This line did not carry passenger trains and the signal box controlled the swing bridge over the Gloucester and Berkeley ship canal. The banner signal close to the signal box regulated canal traffic. Banner signals such as this were to be found in use up to the end of the steam era. The Midland Railway four lever ground frame, in the foreground is protected by a wooden shelter.**
NRM Derby Collection DY10185

Not all signal boxes were covered by the block telegraph system. Whilst these were few in number when compared to the total number of boxes, they are important within the overall scheme of things. These boxes often controlled the movements within marshalling yards, goods stations or even in large locomotive sheds. Others were found on lines that did not carry passenger traffic, such as Canal Bridge box at Gloucester, illustrated on the previous page.

Signal boxes controlling passenger trains were subject to the rigorous regulation. The signalman was guided by the block telegraph, his own vision and apparatus that supplemented or replaced his vision such as fouling bars and track circuits. There were a few signal boxes where there were no siding connections, crossovers or junctions. These boxes were originally opened to shorten block sections in areas where traffic was heavy. Sometimes, if traffic was light, these boxes were switched out, with all their signals left in the clear position. When they were switched out it meant that the block section was made longer. The prime objective in switching out a box was to save the cost of a signalman's wages when the level of traffic permitted a longer than normal block section to be used. There were also cases of signal boxes only being opened for a short period when, for example, the daily freight train was shunting at the station.

The majority of block posts fulfiled the dual function of spacing following trains on the same line and affording protection from crossing or converging movements. The signalman in charge of a block post shared this responsibility with the signalmen at the other end of each section, one in the rear, the other in advance, maintaining communication by means of the block telegraph and later also by telephone.

Under normal circumstances the signalman had to be able to see the track within his yard and therefore the view from the signal box was an important matter. The signal box had to be placed so that from it there would be a view of the whole of the running lines it controlled. The signalman had to have an uninterrupted view from the point at which a train waiting at the first stop signal (on every running line) would come to a stand, up to the signal which allowed entry to the next section. He also had to be able to see the track in bay and platform lines or other subsidiary roads not forming part of the block section, but onto which he might turn trains. Finally, he had to be able to see all the points on, and those leading to, the running lines. Any signals not visible from the signal box had to have electrical repeaters in the box indicating their aspects and thus allowing the signalman to see how they were set.

If we look at this from a modeller's point of view, we find that some very clear rules have been laid down regarding where the signal box should be placed in relation to the section of track it controls. Many modellers use a signal box which is the wrong size for the number of

levers that would be there, if this were a full size installation and not a model. This is probably due to the limited number of kits which are available and a lack of understanding of what dictated the size of a signal box. Research into the number of levers that would be worked from your signal box is essential. This should include provision for levers for signals such as distant, outer home or advanced starting signals that are not located in the area that is being modelled, but which would, if this were a full size railway, be worked from your signal box. This will give you a good idea of the size of the frame and hence the size of signal box that you need to model.

The Board of Trade laid down the limit at which points could be worked from a signal box, and over the years these distances increased. For example, the distance in 1910 for facing points was 250 yards and 300 yards for trailing points. These distances were greater than those allowed in the late nineteenth century and enabled a reduction in the number of signal boxes to be made. As a result of these regulations the layout of many yards practically fixed the position of the signal box, although if the distances were too great then ground frames, locked from the signal box, were employed. This arrangement has potential for modellers who may wish to model the signal box off stage and just reproduce the ground frame on their model. For example if space is limited, but there is a need for a connection to a siding from the running lines, the signal box could be assumed to be out of view and only the ground frame controlling the connection need be modelled.

The signal box was kept as close to the running lines as possible, so that the signalman could observe passing trains for defects or doors not properly closed on passenger trains. In particular the signalman had to see that the tail lamp on a train was in place. If there was no tail lamp on the last vehicle, the train might have split, leaving some vehicles obstructing the section. If a signal box controlled a level crossing, then it was advantageous to locate the box as close to the gates as possible. This meant that the signalman did not have to leave his box for long if the gates had to be opened and closed manually. If the gates were mechanically operated from inside the signal box, it was essential to have the box adjacent to the gates.

The height of the signal box was determined by the need to obtain a good all-round view taking into account adjacent bridges or other obstructions. Very high boxes were disliked on the grounds of expense, but also because they were affected more by foggy conditions. According to Byles in, *The First Principles of Railway Signalling*, 'in the pre-block days it was customary to build very high signal boxes, probably to ensure that the signalman had the best possible view of the line, but the advent of the block system made this unnecessary although some very tall signal boxes remained in service'.

Though the idea of maintaining a space rather than time interval between following trains originated as far back as the the 1850s, some 20 or more years were to pass before the block system had been adopted to any great extent by the major British railway companies. In truth, any system of working that sought to maintain an interval of space between following trains may be described as a block system. It is worth noting that while the 1889 Regulation of Railways Act refers to, 'the block system', it does not define it. A rather more precise description will be found in a publication produced by the LMS entitled, *Book of Instructions to Station Masters: Absolute Block System,* 'the object of Absolute Block Signalling is to prevent more than one train being in a block section between two signal boxes on the same line at the same time'.

The regulations required that a separate block instrument was provided for each road. Later, when telephones were introduced, they were used to assist with communications between the signal box and the District Control Office and others responsible for working trains. Telephones were not used to work the block system.

By the early years of the twentieth century most of the railway companies in the British Isles were using a standard set of block telegraph regulations and codes which were known as the Railway Clearing House Regulations. These had been agreed by representatives of the railway companies working in conjunction with the Railway Clearing House. There were variations in the type of instruments used for block signalling. Some companies used two position instruments, though the three position block instrument may be considered as being the British standard. The Railway Clearing House regulations referred to above related to three position block instruments.

On the full size railway safety was paramount and this was the reason why block signalling was introduced. As this is not a consideration for modellers, much of the minutiae of the regulations and their application is thus irrelevant for the modeller. It is probably best to pick out a few aspects of the practices surrounding block signalling which can be seen and which are thus worth representing on a model railway. One visible manifestation is the necessity of having a tail lamp on trains. Without a tail lamp on the last vehicle, the signalman had to assume that part of the train had been left behind in the section. How many model train formations have we seen breaking this basic rule of operating practice?

The strict principle of space interval working was usually relaxed only in connection with movements in which non-passenger trains were involved. The principle was modified to the extent of allowing more than one train in the same section at the same time. This was known as permissive block working and its use was usually restricted to lines used exclu-

Right: **This diagram shows a typical arrangement of a locking frame and its connections to the levers in a signal box.**

Below: **Signal boxes were found in all sorts of locations including station platforms as will be see from this 1950s view of Nantybwch No 1. This junction station was located where the former LNWR Heads of the Valleys line was met by that company's branch serving the Sirhowy valley. By this date ex-Great Western locomotives were working on this ex-LNWR line. 64XX 0-6-0 pannier tank No 6426 has arrived with an auto train from Tredegar.** Lens of Sutton

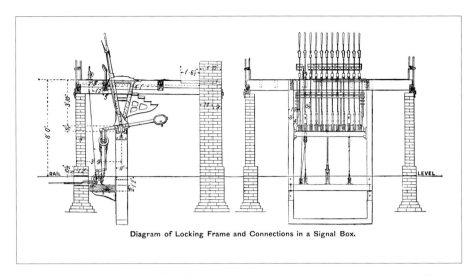

Diagram of Locking Frame and Connections in a Signal Box.

sively for non-passenger traffic. Permissive working was used to a very limited extent, under special circumstances, on passenger lines. An example of this would be where one train was allowed to slowly approach another train at a platform in a station.

Under permissive block working, which allowed trains to enter a section already occupied, each train was stopped, or slowed down to a crawl by the signalman keeping the stop signal at danger until the train had nearly come to a stand at the entrance to the section. My recollection of this method of working was that we would know we were going to run up to the rear of another train by the fact that the signal had been kept at danger and that as we approached the signal box, the signalman appeared in view. He would hold up his hand, his fingers indicating to the driver the number of trains ahead of him so that he would be prepared to stop as required. The method of signalling used in circumstances of permissive block working, was similar to that used in absolute block working except that a train could be offered to the box ahead while the block indicator still showed, 'train on line'.

During my days as a fireman it was not unusual to see as many as five freight trains, nose to tail, on both the Up goods line between Kings Norton and Northfield and on the Down goods line between Washwood Heath and Castle Bromwich. It was normal practice for the second train to almost buffer up to the brake van of the first train and so on down the line. This enabled the driver and fireman to join the guard in his van. It was always more comfortable in a brake van than in the engine cab, in particular on a cold winter night.

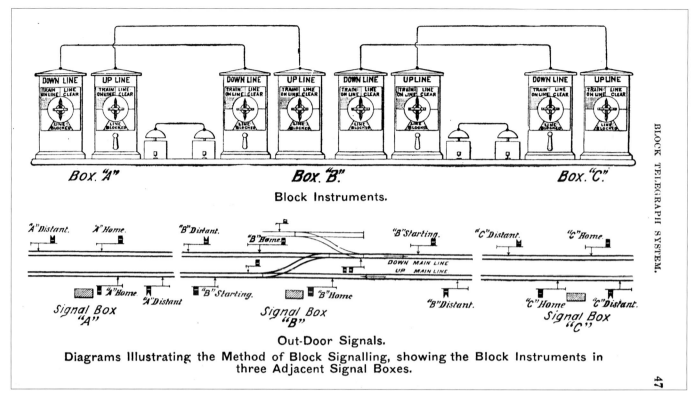

Block Instruments.

Out-Door Signals.

Diagrams Illustrating the Method of Block Signalling, showing the Block Instruments in three Adjacent Signal Boxes.

BLOCK TELEGRAPH SYSTEM.

47

CODE OF TERMS AND REGULATIONS APPLICABLE TO BLOCK TELEGRAPH WORKING ON DOUBLE LINES OF RAILWAY.
BELL SIGNALS.

REGU-LATION NUMBER.	DESCRIPTION OF SIGNAL.		HOW TO BE GIVEN.
1	CALL ATTENTION SIGNAL		1
	Passenger Train or Breakdown Van Train not going to clear the Line.	Main Line ... Branch ...	3 pause 1 1 pause 3
	Breakdown Van Train going to clear the Line, or Light Engine going to assist disabled Train.	Main Line ... Branch ...	2 pause 2 4 pause 4
	Fish, Meat, Fruit, Horse, Cattle, Milk or Perishable Train composed of coaching stock.	Main Line ... Branch ...	4 pause 2 pause 2 2 pause 2 pause 4
3 & 4	Is LINE CLEAR for Empty Train	Main Line ... Branch ...	2 pause 2 pause 1 1 pause 2 pause 2
	Goods or Through Ballast Train or Engines and Brakes	Main Line ... Branch ...	3 pause 2 2 pause 3
	Light Engine or Light Engines coupled together ...	Main Line ... Branch ...	4 pause 1 1 pause 4
3, 4 & 8	Is LINE CLEAR for Ballast Train requiring to stop in Section or Goods Train Working at intermediate Sidings		5 consecutively
3, 4 & 9	Is LINE CLEAR for Trolley requiring to pass through Tunnel		2 pause 2 pause 2
3, 4 & 9A	Is LINE CLEAR for Power-worked Inspection Car or mechanically or power-worked Trolley.	Through ... Required to stop in Section	1 pause 1 pause 1 1 pause 3 pause 1
3	TRAIN ENTERING SECTION	Main Line ... Branch ...	2 consecutively 4 consecutively
5	SECTION CLEAR BUT STATION OR JUNCTION BLOCKED		3 pause 5 pause 5
6	BANK ENGINE IN REAR OF TRAIN		1 pause 4 pause 1
10 & 12	TRAIN OUT OF SECTION OR OBSTRUCTION REMOVED		2 pause 1
10A	ENGINE ARRIVED		2 pause 1 pause 3
	TRAIN DRAWN BACK CLEAR OF SECTION		3 pause 2 pause 3
11	TRAIN AN UNUSUALLY LONG TIME IN SECTION		6 pause 2
12	OBSTRUCTION DANGER		6 consecutively
13	BLOCKING BACK	Inside Home Signal ... Outside Home Signal ...	2 pause 4 3 pause 3
17	STOP AND EXAMINE TRAIN		7 consecutively
18	CANCELLING " IS LINE CLEAR ? " or " TRAIN ENTERING SECTION " SIGNAL ...		3 pause 5
	LAST TRAIN SIGNALLED INCORRECTLY DESCRIBED		5 pause 3
19	TRAIN PASSED WITHOUT TAIL LAMP	To Box in Advance ... To Box in Rear ...	9 consecutively 4 pause 5
20	TRAIN DIVIDED		5 pause 5
21	SHUNT TRAIN FOR FOLLOWING TRAIN TO PASS		1 pause 5 pause 5
22	VEHICLES RUNNING AWAY ON WRONG LINE		2 pause 5 pause 5
23	VEHICLES RUNNING AWAY ON RIGHT LINE		4 pause 5 pause 5
24	OPENING OF SIGNAL BOX		5 pause 5 pause 5
	CLOSING OF SIGNAL BOX		7 pause 5 pause 5
27	TESTING BLOCK INDICATORS AND BELLS		16 consecutively

Above: This drawing illustrates the relationship between three adjacent signal boxes. The first thing to note is that there is a separate block instrument for each line in each box. A and C are simple block posts whereas B has a more complex arrangement including a siding, a crossover and both home and starting signals in each direction. Though each running line has a separate instrument there was only one bell for communication between the boxes. This will have to be used to convey information on both lines.

Left: It is important to remember that the main method of communication between block posts was by bell code. Not only was this a quicker method of communication than using the telephone, it eliminated the possibility of misunderstandings which could have arisen during the course of a conversation. A correctly given bell code could only mean one thing. This is an extract from the Southern Railway listing of bell signals applicable to block telegraph working on double lines of railway. The bell codes used by the Big Four varied, but the codes were standardised by British Railways in the early 1950s.

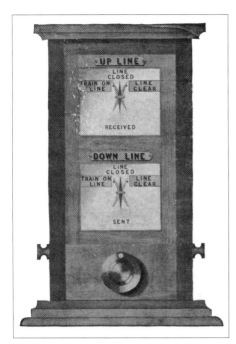

Above: **This is a typical three position block instrument that was used on the British railway system. I have seen models of this type of equipment, in a simplified form, in use on model railways to good effect. It adds immensely to the realism of train working.**

Top right: **Signal boxes come in all shapes, sizes and locations. Some companies used standard designs, on other lines there was much greater diversity. Highbridge East box, on the former Somerset & Dorset Joint line, recorded here in July 1962, will represent for us the smaller signal box. Its frame was only big enough for 12 levers, the platform at the foot of the steps coming down from the entrance to the cabin, was for staff exchange purposes. Not all signal boxes were located beside running lines like the examples on this page, some could also be found at goods stations, marshalling yards and engine sheds.**
Paul Cottrell

Bottom right: **The design and style of signal boxes varied considerably. Some were designed by the owning company, others were made to the signalling contractors' own designs. The box at Haltwhistle, junction for the branch to Alston, on the old North Eastern Railway's Newcastle to Carlisle line, was photographed in September 1963. The great height of the box was due to the adjacent footbridge. The signalman had to see over this to get a complete view of his yard. Another interesting feature of this box is that the rods which operated the points and signals run down vertically outside the front of the box.** Hugh Oliver

Above: **This model of Dewsbury was built in 4mm scale to 00 Finescale track standards by members of the Manchester Model Railway Society. An example of a railway in an industrial setting, it is correctly signalled throughout and this adds greatly to the realism of the layout. In this view,**

Black 5 No 44753, a member of the class fitted with Caprotti valve gear, has clear signals at the head of a fully fitted express freight train, or as enginemen would say, she 'has the road'.

Below: **The bracket signals are a prominent feature of this other view of Dewsbury which shows WD 2-8-0 No 90001 shunting goods wagons at the station.**
Both, Tony Wright

TRAFFIC

Some modellers choose to replicate an actual location though they may, for various reasons, generally lack of space, foreshorten this or omit certain features. Modellers who follow this path need to establish what happened at the place they are modelling and while this can be difficult if an obscure location is chosen, it is not impossible to discover what traffic would have been seen there in the period being modelled.

Many other modellers focus on railways that either did not exist or were planned but never built. This can make life more complicated or rewarding, depending upon your attitude to research and level of accuracy that you seek. All railways were built to generate revenue for the shareholders by making a profit from the business of transport provision. Therefore if you plan to model a railway that was not built, the starting point has to be to try and establish what sort of traffic it would have dealt with, had it been constructed. It is important to get this right at the outset. Some modellers choose a location which would never have had much traffic even in its heyday and then have to invent all manner of highly unrealistic trains to run through it to widen its interest.

Almost inevitably, my remarks about traffic patterns are fairly general in their nature. It would be impossible to comment in detail on changing traffic flows across the network over many decades. Therefore, I have decided to concentrate on some of the traffic which would have been carried in that period which is still the most popular one for modellers, the years from the late 1930s up to the 1950s.

Let us begin with passenger traffic. This is fairly straightforward as it covers the transportation of people by passenger train and the conveyance of certain types of goods on passenger trains. The latter could include parcels, livestock and general merchandise. Items of goods conveyed by passenger trains generated a higher rate of revenue for the railway company than if it were conveyed by a goods train. This included general parcels traffic, a term used to describe small parcels that went by passenger train. Newspapers, periodicals and perishables were all rated under the broad heading of passenger traffic, even if they did not travel in a passenger train.

At one time milk was taken in churns to the station from whence it was conveyed in the brake compartment of a coach in a passenger train. If there was a lot of milk to transport, then it would be carried in a separate vehicle that formed part of the passenger train. Although the vehicle did not carry passengers, if it was included in the formation of a passenger train, its suspension, couplings, drawgear and brakes had to be to passenger stock standards. The railway companies classified vehicles that could run in passenger trains, but did not carry passengers as, non passenger coaching or carrying stock. In addition to milk, other traffic that could be conveyed by passenger trains included, fish, fruit and vegetables, butter, eggs and meat.

There were of course a huge variety of types of passenger train from main line expresses to crowded commuter trains and branch line services ambling along country by-ways. Modellers will know from the nature of the location they are modelling what sort of passenger trains they can run on their layouts. If they have any doubts, a brief bit of research in the public or working timetables for the period in which their model is set, will quickly establish the sort of passenger trains they should be running, and their frequency. Special passenger traffic can also be introduced. If they can make a connection between their location and a port, perhaps special boat trains, running at irregular intervals to connect with ocean liners, can be appear from time to time. Excursions, football specials and troop trains are all options which can be explored and added to the basic passenger service on a layout.

If passenger traffic is relatively straightforward, when it come to considering the variety of goods traffic which was carried by the railways, the complexity and interest of the subject is almost infinite. Up to the end of the Great War, the railways had a virtual monopoly of the land carriage of bulk goods traffic in Great Britain. Even though from 1919 onwards, with the increasing availability of motor vehicles, the railways began to loose traffic to the roads, in the late 1930s the extent of the average railway wagon journey was less than 40 miles for coal and coke traffic and 70 miles for merchandise which suggests that the railways still handled a considerable amount of local and short haul traffic. In this part of the book we will explore some of the main traffic flows carried by rail looking at these on both a geographical and an industry by industry basis. This may assist those who want to build fictional layouts set in particular areas to judge the sorts of traffic which their wagons could be conveying. We will begin with the traffic which the agricultural industry brought to the railways.

Today with most foods available virtually all year round, it is easy to forget that in previous decades there was an important seasonal element to food distribution with the railways being called on to deal with certain types of traffic at different times of the year. A good example of this was the carriage of potatoes. In the late 1930s the production of potatoes, not counting those grown in gardens and allotments, was about 4½ million tons per annum. The principle producing areas were largely in the eastern part of the country and included the districts surrounding The Wash and the Humber, North Yorkshire and Durham. Although some potatoes were transported in bulk, much of the production was bagged before distribution to retailers. The sacks were usually carried in open wagons that were sheeted over, although vans could also be used. The traffic in home-grown potatoes was seasonal, mainly from September to March. Outside this period there was a considerable traffic in imported potatoes which was generally conveyed in bags.

An immense traffic in fruit and vegetables was at at one time carried by rail, using both goods and passenger trains. A few examples of such traffic flows will have to suffice. Strawberries from the continent came from the port of Brest to Plymouth from where they were conveyed by special trains to Bristol, going forward from there to destinations in the Midlands and the north of England. Other imported fruit came via Dover. Wagons were worked northwards over the Metropolitan Widened Lines to north London yards where they were remarshalled before going forward in fitted express freight trains.

Fruit and vegetables from the eastern counties were dispatched to a number of destinations, with a regular flows going to London, Liverpool and Manchester. Tomatoes grown in the Channel Islands came into Weymouth. From there wagons would go to places like Banbury and Woodford, where they were remarshalled before going forward to destinations such as Hull, Sheffield, Darlington, Dundee and Aberdeen . Much of this traffic was carried in covered goods vans but tarpaulin sheeted open goods wagons were also used. At peak periods other vehicles were pressed into service. One quite well known example is the use of cattle wagons to bring Cornish broccoli to market in London.

Perishable traffic like this had to be moved quickly in fitted freight trains that would require suitable wagons with oil axleboxes and with the required percentage of vehicles in the train equipped with the automatic vacuum brake. Grain was conveyed in sacks, often owned by the railway companies. It was loaded into open wagons that were sheeted over. The railway companies built some dedicated hopper grain wagons but even so the bulk of the traffic was carried in merchandise wagons. In addition to grain, there was a considerable tonnage of milling offals to be moved from the individual mills for distribution elsewhere.

Livestock was another major source of traffic which the agricultural industry brought to the railways. Most of this consisted of cattle, sheep and pigs; the numbers of horses and goats conveyed were small in comparison. There was an important import trade in livestock from Ireland through west coast ports such as Holyhead, Heysham, and Stranraer, which were served by LMS operated steamers. Often the animals were carried in special cattle trains worked from the port of entry through to their final destination.

In addition to the Irish livestock traffic there were a considerable internal movements of livestock throughout Great Britain. Beef cattle were produced in the eastern counties, Yorkshire, Northants and Warwickshire, while diary cattle came from areas like Cheshire, Cumber-

Top: **This view, showing the interior of St Philips goods station in Bristol in 1922, speaks eloquently of the vast range of general merchandise conveyed by the railways in their heyday. It underlines what goods traffic was all about in the steam era and demonstrates something of the diversity of loads that were carried by rail at this time.**

Above: **Barnetby station was on the Great Central line between Grimsby and Gainsborough in Lincolnshire. There are milk churns on the platform and barrows** to deal with the parcels and other goods which would have been in the guard's van of most passenger trains calling at the station. This clutter, churns, parcels, barrows and the rest, was an essential part of the station scene as recorded in many photographs of busy station platforms in the days of steam. Some model platforms are far too tidy to be realistic, modellers should reproduce the apparent chaos that was to be seen.

Opposite page: **Railways were but one part, albeit an important one, of a broader** transport picture. Here at Avon Wharf in Bristol, road, rail and water transport come together to provide a splendid panorama full of interesting detail. Not just the railway wagons, but the canal barges are owned by the Midland Railway. Horses are being used for shunting. Note the narrow berth for the barges, the short rail sidings, the wooden stop blocks and the steam crane with its coal supply. Though there is not a steam locomotive to be seen, this scene could form the basis for a fascinating model. NRM Derby Collection DY 1025

land, Shropshire and Buckinghamshire and sheep were raised from the Scottish Borders down to Kent and Sussex. Domestic cattle movements included relatively short trips between rural stations and country towns and the big cities where much of the beef was processed and consumed. There was also a considerable movement between market towns as a result of dealers selling and buying livestock. Finally there were the annual sheep sales that saw many sheep being moved from Scotland, Wales and southern England to farms in the Midlands. It is easy to forget the importance of this traffic to the railways as all of it has been been lost to the roads for such a long time.

Cattle wagons were originally classified as being either 'large' 18ft inside, 'medium' 15ft 6in inside or 'small' 13ft 6in inside. The large wagons could be partitioned off to carry less than a full load of livestock. This led to the withdrawal of the two smaller sizes so that by the 1930s they were virtually extinct. Many cattle wagons were built with automatic brakes or through brake pipes and some were fitted with steam pipes to permit their use at the head of passenger trains.

The manufacture of bricks and tiles was carried on at various locations throughout the country where suitable deposits of clay were available. Depending upon the clay used, a number of different varieties of bricks and tiles were made. There is a clay seam that extends across the country from The Wash to the Bristol Channel. Other major deposits exist in South Staffordshire and north east Lancashire.

There was a demand for bricks and tiles throughout the United Kingdom. They were often conveyed in containers with straw used as a packing material, otherwise they were carried in open wagons. A crane would be required to remove the loaded container from the wagon at its destination. The LNER constructed bogie wagons for bricks. These had to be unloaded by hand in the goods yard.

Another building material carried by rail was cement. During the late 1930s the total production of cement was in excess of 5 million tons. The location of the cement works depended upon the availability of raw materials. Major works included those at Hope, Clitheroe and Purfleet. Cement was transported in paper bags loaded into covered goods vans. Upon arrival at its destination the

cement was often stored at works with private sidings or in warehouses on railway premises.

An enormous volume of chemicals was moved by rail. Heavy chemicals, included acids for manufacturing purposes, alkalies and fertilisers. Other products rated as chemicals were, those used for medicinal and laboratory purposes, coal tar distillation products, dyestuffs, explosives, fats, greases, soaps, disinfectants, insecticides, glues, paints and resins.

In addition to the dispatch of the finished products of the chemical industry, the raw materials were brought to the factories by rail and large tonnage of coal was required for the factory boilers. Long trainloads of coal and limestone were a notable feature of this traffic. Many chemicals are dangerous to handle being corrosive, poisonous or explosive. Some were conveyed in private owners' tank wagons or metal drums, cylinders or glass carboys. Though a number of the chemical works were connected to canals, the bulk of industry's transport needs were met by rail, Many chemical works had their own sidings and often their own locomotives to handle the internal traffic. Such facilities offer excellent opportunities for the modeller.

Hardware and holloware were largely produced in the Midlands together with the Bristol and Sheffield areas. The products were varied and so was the method of distribution. Some items such as dustbins were not packed, while spades and shovels were tied in bundles. Most products were packed into boxes, wooden cases, crates or hampers. They were conveyed in open wagons sheeted over or in covered vans. Covered containers were also often used for this class of traffic.

The railway companies classified the traffic in inflammable liquids according to their flash point. Crude benzol, crude coal tar naphtha, crude petroleum or shale oil for refining, benzine, motor spirit and petroleum were classified as 'A'. Others, for example gas oil, white spirit and burning oils were class 'B'.

The bulk of the traffic consisted of crude oil being taken into the refineries and fuel for internal combustion engines leaving them. The product was carried in owners' tank wagons with a 12/14-ton carrying capacity, built to standard specifications. When the loaded tank wagons arrived at their destinations, often adjacent to goods yards, the contents of the tank wagons were pumped into large storage tanks. From these it was transferred, as required, into road tankers which took the fuel to the end users. These rail connected storage and distribution points offer modelling potential for small industrial layouts.

At the core of Britain's traditional manufacturing industry was iron and steel production. The fortunes of this industry were closely interwoven with those of the railways companies and offer considerable modelling opportunities. The traffic from this industry can be divided into five categories; iron ore, pig iron, blooms, billets and ingots, iron and steel scrap and manufactured products.

Iron ore was used in blast furnaces, where it was mixed with other materials, such as limestone, to produce pig iron. Iron ore was both mined or quarried in certain parts of Britain or imported. Pig iron was used in foundries for the manufacture of cast or wrought iron products, most of which today would be made of plastic. Factories producing this type of product were located throughout Britain though they were concentrated in certain areas, such as the Black Country. These products were generally carried in open merchandise wagons.

Blooms, billets, ingots and steel bars were produced after the pig iron had been converted into iron or steel. Production was generally in the Midlands, northern England and the Glasgow, Ayr and Swansea areas. The movement of this traffic often required the use of what the railway companies described as, 'specially constructed wagons', such as bogie bolsters, flat trucks and well trolleys.

Iron and steel scrap came from such places as iron and steel works, engineering and motor factories, municipal salvage depots and ship breakers and amounted to a very considerable tonnage per year. In addition, scrap was

imported, mostly through ports on the east coast. This traffic was widespread across many parts of the United Kingdom and was carried in open goods wagons.

Manufactured iron and steel products offer a wide range of possibilities to modellers who wish to include interesting loads in their wagons. The products within this category included anchors, cables and chain, girders, guttering and roofing, hoop iron, pipes, plates, rails, tubes, castings, forgings, wire and wheels. Some of these products were carried in open goods wagons, but others required special wagons. For example, large steel plates were often conveyed in bogie wagons fitted with a trestle whilst steel tubes were carried in long open wagons specifically designed for this class of traffic. Some of these loads could be out of gauge. If they were, special arrangements had to be made, which could include wrong line working and this often took place on a Sunday, when traffic was light.

At the other end of a scale of fragility from iron and steel, was paper and related products such as strawboard and fibreboard. These were made from mainly imported raw materials like wood pulp and esparto grass, together with waste paper and other recycled materials. Although most of the raw material was imported through the east coast ports a considerable tonnage came via ports on the Mersey, Clyde and Severn rivers. Other raw material was domestic in origin, china clay being the most distinctive from the standpoint of modellers. Large quantities of water is required for paper making, which helps to explain why paper mills, which were found throughout Britain were often located close to rivers or canals.

Road making materials were frequently carried by rail. The principle materials within this category were granite, limestone, gravel and slag. Prior to the Second World War, cement represented only a small proportion of the material used. These products, which were carried in open wagons, were found throughout the country. Many of the producers and the customers for this material, were rail connected.

Works producing sanitary tubes were frequently located in areas where the raw material used, clay, was to be found. A large quantity of coal was required for firing the kilns used in the industry. The numerous companies engaged in this trade were to be found across the country in Staffordshire, Yorkshire, Lancashire, Ayrshire, South Wales, Kent, Sussex and Gloucestershire. The finished tubes were carried in open wagons, including the special shock absorbing type that reduced the possibility of damage to such fragile products. Open containers were also used with heather, straw or similar materials used to protect the pipes from damage.

During the late 1930s consumption of sugar in the United Kingdom was about 2.5 million tons per annum. About three quarters of this was made from imported sugar cane. The

remainder was produced from home grown sugar beet. Most of the imports came through Liverpool and London, but the ports of Greenock, Hull, Bristol and Manchester handled about 20% of the total tonnage. A lot of the home produced sugar beet was grown in the eastern counties where many of the sugar refineries were to be found. These refineries used large quantities of coal and limestone as well, which also came in by rail. In addition to the sugar, there was outward traffic in the by-products of the industry such as molasses, beet pulp and spent lime. The latter was used by farmers.

The textile industry had played a significant role in the British economy since the eighteenth century. The industry needed vast quantities of wool and cotton. Less than 25% of the wool required by the industry was home produced. The textile industry was concentrated in Lancashire, the West Riding of Yorkshire and in the Scottish borders. Apart from the wool and cotton, large quantities of water and coal to power the boilers of the mills were required. The raw materials, both home produced and imported, were usually carried in open wagons.

Prior to the Great War, the Lancashire cotton industry dominated the world market, but in the years that followed, cheaper products, mostly made in Japan, adversely affected the British export trade. The imported raw cotton chiefly arrived at Liverpool or Manchester. Some went direct from ship to mill though large quantities were stored in warehouses prior to being sent to the mills.

Hosiery is knitted wear and the principle areas of production were in Leicestershire, Nottinghamshire, Derbyshire and around Dumfries and Hawick in Scotland. Most of the yarn came from the West Riding, but some materials were imported. Finished products was usually in small consignments and were shipped by both goods and passenger services. From a modelling standpoint cartons, boxes and small bales can represent this traffic.

Timber traffic carried on the railways can be divided between home grown and imported timber. Although most trees were felled during the winter months, the transporting of timber was carried on throughout the year. Timber was moved to the sawmills in the round and special vehicles were used. The trade in timber, which was carried by rail, was vast and ranged from large trees to manufactured timber products such as pit props. The large coal mining industry used great quantities of these, many of which were imported. These were were often seen being transported in open goods wagons from the ports. Specialty timber, not native to Britain, had to be imported. This traffic often went to receivers with private sidings and timber-stacking areas at goods stations were not uncommon.

Whilst all of the foregoing traffic flows, and others which we have not had the space to mention, were important for the railways, it was the conveyance of minerals that formed by

Right: **One of the great advances in the handling of rail borne goods came with the widespread introduction of containers from the mid 1920s onwards. This picture shows an early LMS container being loaded onto a horse drawn dray. There is again much of modelling interest here. The fixed revolving crane was a feature of many goods yards. There is a lot of room between the sidings to allow the crane to operate and to permit access by road vehicles. Note how the surface of the area used by road vehicles has been built up to rail level.**
NRM Derby Collection DY 13876

Below: **Weigh bridges were very common and were to be found at even quite small goods stations. The weigh bridge, with its office and distinctive cast iron deck, was always placed close to the exit from the goods yard. This picture was taken at Camden and has the usual arrangement for the bridge and a large office beside it, appropriate for such an obviously busy location.**

far the greatest part of the volume of goods carried on Britain's railways. The biggest component of this was coal. Coal was the principal fuel used in Britain for most of the age of steam. Along with iron, its easy availability, formed the basis of the industrial prosperity of the country. In the inter war years, between 200 and 250 million tons of coal was mined per year, with about 20% of this of this being exported.

Any model of the steam era railway must take this into account. Coal was used to generate electricity and make gas as well as being being applied directly in a multitude of locations to create heat or steam. Whilst there were coalfields all over Britain, from Scotland down to Kent, the greatest concentration of coal mines were to be found in Northumberland, Durham, Yorkshire, Nottinghamshire, Derbyshire and South Wales. Smaller coalfields were also found in Cumberland, Lancashire, Cheshire, North Wales, Staffordshire, Leicestershire, Shropshire, the Forest of Dean, Mon-mouthshire and Somerset. Few places in mainland Britain that were far from a coalfield.

Not all coal traffic was moved by rail. In 1937 more than twice as much coal came to London by sea than was carried by rail and several million tons went to other ports in Great Britain. Often it was cheaper to send coal by sea than by rail, or to use rail for just part of the journey.

Almost all collieries had private siding accommodation. It was common for coal to be loaded into wagons and held for storage until it was sold. When trade was slack this could cause congestion when the collieries did not have room for empty wagons because their internal sidings were full. The main customers of the collieries, gas works, power stations, steel plants and chemical factories, all had their own private sidings, often shunted by their own locomotives.

Before both the coal mines and the railways were nationalised after the Second World War, in England and Wales, with the exception of coal for railway use, much railborne coal was carried in wagons not owned by the railway companies. These wagons could be owned by the collieries, coal merchants, the various industrial works such as gas or electricity producers who used large quantities of coal, or the coal factors, the wholesalers who handled a vast tonnage each year. Railway enthusiasts call these, private owners wagons, but before the war, the usual railway description omitted the word private. In Scotland where greater use was made of railway company wagons, there were far fewer owners wagons to be seen.

This brief and far from comprehensive survey I hope demonstrates just how important goods traffic, especially the carriage of minerals, was to the railways during the age of steam and how much potential and variety there is for the modeller in running goods trains on his layout replicating the traffic patterns applicable to the area in which the layout is set, goods trains that is with realistic loads in the correct type of goods vehicles for that traffic.

Left and above: **These are examples of goods and mineral traffic wagon labels. They were attached to the wagon by a spring clip and provided information as to the destination and the route the wagon was to take to get there.**

Below left: **Old, time expired vans and coaches, were given a new lease of life when they were used as mobile or, as in this picture, static warehouses. This picture, taken at Llanrwst & Trefriw on the Conway Valley branch in the early 1950s, shows an ex-LNWR passenger brake van in use as a store.** J Moss

Opposite page, top: **Large goods stations were to be found in all the major cities and provincial towns throughout Great Britain. A common feature was that they generally were several floors high as land values in urban areas meant that it was cheaper to build upwards than outwards. The upper floors were reached by lifts or hoists, seen here on the outside of the Midland depot at Leicester, which was photographed in 1922.** NRM Derby Collection DY12760

Opposite page, bottom: **Any modeller who wishes to lay out a marshalling yard should study this picture, taken at Wellingborough in 1894. In front of the camera are two fans of sidings, six to the left and five to the right. Access to the sidings is provided by four three throw points, all of which are different, and a single point on the left. The point levers are in four groups of two and a single lever to the left. The temporary shelters for the shunters suggest that they maybe working some distance from a shunters cabin. Many modellers ballast their sidings to main line standards. This picture shows that it was more usual for the ground area to be raised to the top of the sleepers. The raised path between the two sets of point levers is another interesting aspect of the scene.** NRM Derby Collection DY 613

Above: **This pre-grouping view of the Midland marshalling yards at Toton demonstrates the vital importance of coal traffic to the railways. Lines of loaded or empty coal wagons stretch as far as the eye can see. In addition to the Midland's own wagons many owner wagons can be seen in the picture**

Centre left: **China clay, used in the paper and ceramics industries, has been conveyed by rail for many years. The china clay is found in Cornwall where it is still an important traffic flow for the railway. Distinctive whitened China clay wagons are also features on many models of Cornish branch lines. Here, former GWR 0-6-0 pannier tank No 9673 hauls a train of china clay wagons, all covered with tarpaulin sheets, on the Fowey branch.**
N Fields

Bottom left: **Many modellers are attracted to light railways such as the erstwhile Kent & East Sussex Railway. It is not hard to see why, as these lines allow mixed trains, such as the one pictured here, to be run. This view, was taken at Rolvenden, about half way along the line, in July 1952. The locomotive is an ex South Eastern Railway 0-6-0. The train is made up of a third brake carriage, one covered goods van, six merchandise wagons and a 20ton goods brake van.** T J Edgington

Right: **The pictures on this page illustrate how some modellers have tackled the portrayal of aspects of goods traffic on their layouts. Dartley is a model of a small rural GWR station where livestock traffic would have been important. In this picture we can see a rake of cattle wagons being shunted. The siding and the loading bay are not long enough to enable many wagons to be loaded or unloaded at the same time. As could easily have been the case on a full sized railway, a few cattle wagons will be shunted into position at the dock and then moved out of the way to enable other wagons to be dealt with.** Tony Wright

Centre right: **The absence of life suggests a meal break at this industrial scene on Ufford, a 4mm scale model. A full size example of the type of motive power pictured on this layout, can be seen on page 12.** Tony Wright

Below: **This north facing view of Heckmondwike shows an ex Midland Railway 0-6-0 No 3175 with an Engineers' train, whose ballast brake is hidden behind the signal and telegraph post. When the picture was taken business was slack, there is little sign of activity in the goods yard. For some reason unknown to me, engineering trains are rarely modelled. This is a pity as they often included some rather interesting vehicles.**
Courtesy, North London Group

PASSENGER STATIONS

As I have stated before, I strongly believe that as far as track layouts are concerned, modellers should seek their inspiration from the prototype. Having stated that, the track layouts reproduced in this part of the book were first drawn to be used as teaching examples at the LMS School of Transport. They do not therefore relate to particular locations, rather they were produced to demonstrate the features which were being taught. As such they were useful as teaching aids for the LMS and they will serve the same purpose here as they show how certain railway moves should be carried out.

However, before considering in detail these LMS classroom examples and the operational practices which they demonstrate, let us remind ourselves of some of the various types of stations that were to be found on the British railway system.

A halt was the simplest and most basic form of station. These were often unmanned, although if they were adjacent to a level crossing, the gatekeeper might have some function in connection with them. Some rudimentary shelter for passengers waiting for trains was

usually provided, lighting, if it was provided at all, was often in the form of an oil lamp. Usually, there was no provision for the handling of goods at halts.

Roadside or country stations were next in terms of their importance. These stations varied in size and would generally have separate good facilities. Depending upon the size of the station and population of the surrounding area, these could range from a single siding, to a yard and a goods shed. There could also be sidings for coal traffic, a cattle dock and an end and side loading dock with a crane.

Moving up the scale to the bigger types of stations, some large suburban stations were similar to halts in that they catered for passenger traffic only and had no goods facilities. On the other hand, larger stations in the provinces would probably have a substantial goods station nearby for both originating and terminating traffic, together with a locomotive shed and possibly carriage sheds or sidings.

Outside of the city termini, some of the most impressive stations where those provided at important junctions. The most famous of these was arguably Crewe, which also boasted two large engine sheds and of course its famous works, as well as extensive goods facilities. At the other end of the scale there were many modest junctions scattered along Britain's main lines where branch lines commenced.

These would have limited passenger and freight facilities and perhaps a single road engine shed or maybe only a turntable for the branch engine.

Terminal stations, irrespective of their size, were generally important places. A terminal station could be anything from a single platform at the end of a country branch line to a major station with numerous platforms in a large city. All the main types of traffic, general goods, minerals and livestock, were accepted at most terminal stations. At the smaller terminal stations, the goods facilities were usually adjacent to the passenger station but at the large city terminals the goods station could be some distance away. These large terminals would also have carriage sheds and a locomotive depot. At some places, Paddington and Kings Cross spring to mind, there were separate facilities to service locomotives close to the station, enabling them to be turned and prepared for a return trip without visiting the locomotive shed. Many of the larger stations grew piecemeal and few British railway stations, which were subject to considerable traffic growth in the past, were entirely ideal as far as track layout was concerned, while some were an operational nightmare.

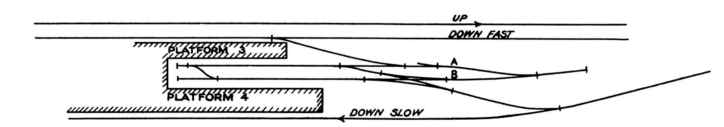

Above: **This is the first track layout shown in the LMS manual and if at first it appears to be slightly confusing, this is probably due to it being a section of a larger drawing. The drawing shows part of a through station with two bay platforms. The text in the manual said: 'The engine of a train arriving in either platform 3 or 4 can be released by running through the crossing, (at the station end of the platform lines), on to the unoccupied platform road, or the train can be disposed of into Sidings 'A' or 'B' by being propelled by the train engine, and the engine subsequently released, leaving both platforms clear for other trains. A train stabled in Sidings 'A' or 'B,' when required for a subsequent service, can be berthed by gravitation and without employing shunting power.'**

The procedure recommended by the LMS

manual presents a problem for modellers trying to replicate this manoeuvre. On the full size railway a guard or shunter, would climb into the coach with the brake compartment and release the handbrake, in order to make the berthing move. By careful use of the handbrake he would control the speed of the coaches and stop short of the buffer stops with the train alongside the platform. Before departure, the engine would back down and be coupled on. Unless there was an electric motor in one of the coaches, this move could not be undertaken on a model. However the track layout does provide an interesting arrangement that could be adapted by modellers. It puts a lot of lines and connections into a small area. A lot of interesting shunting activity could be carried out on a layout such as this.

By rearranging the track layout so that

we have an Up and Down through platform and a bay with two platform faces as shown, we could create a terminus which dealt with branch, or turnback trains, within a through station. The layout would have a facing connection into the bay off the Down line and a connection to the Up line in the trailing position. A scissors crossing would be at the exit end and with the crossover at the station end, the same facilities would be retained. It would also be possible to have one or two carriage sidings between the running lines. They could be arranged as dead end sidings or as shown. Depending upon how they were set out they would probably require trap points, as already exists on siding 'A' in the plan. The sidings on the LMS plan reproduced here are not to scale, they are much too short to hold a train of coaches.

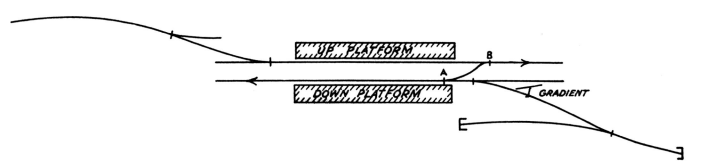

Above: **This is another manoeuvre where gravity shunting is involved. This is rather more complex and not as easy as the example shown on page 52. First the LMS method as to how this should be done:** *'This layout will permit a train arriving in the Down direction to return in the Up direction, although there is only one crossover road. There are two methods of performing this movement:* 1) Owing to the Down line gradient falling towards the station, the engine can be detached at the Down Home signal and run forward beyond the crossover road. The engine is then crossed to the opposite line and the coaches gravitated clear of crossing A-B. The engine is then backed on to the train and the train is drawn through the crossing to the Up line and set back into the station.* 2) After the train has arrived at the Down platform and is clear of the crossing A-B, the train is propelled on to the Up platform road, the engine detached and run to the Down line. The points are then reversed to allow the empty coaches to run by gravitation to the Up platform and the engine run through crossover A-B to the Up line and backed on to the train.'*

Although the LMS manual does not say so, no passengers would be permitted to stay on the train whilst these movements were being made. Shunting by gravity would only be permitted with empty coaching stock.

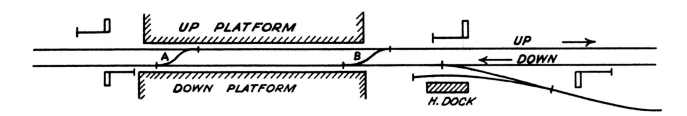

Above: **This was the exercise from the LMS teaching manual move that caused the most interest among my railway friends. Almost without exception, all modellers gave what the LMS considered to be an incorrect answer. On the other hand people involved with preserved railways usually gave the correct answer. My theory, as far as modellers are concerned, is that they prefer to pull rather than propel their rolling stock in order to avoid the possibility of derailments that could be caused by buffer locking and this thinking may have influenced their answers. This plan offers a layout which could form the template for a good model.**

This is what the LMS manual had to say: *'This is a layout that will permit the turnback of a train arriving in the Down or Up platform. There is a facility for detaching or attaching in the horse dock by the train engine. The diagram illustrates the right and wrong methods of running round a train. The wrong method; the coaches of a train arriving at the Down platform are left in the Down platform road. The engine runs round through the crossover roads 'A' and 'B'. The coaches are then propelled along the Down line and drawn through 'A' onto the Up platform.'*

A more common wrong method than the one identified by the LMS, in my view, and one that many modellers would use, is to leave the coaches in the Down platform whilst the engine runs round. It then re-couples to the stock and draws the coaches through crossover 'B', to stop when clear of the points and then to set back into the Up platform. Regardless of the two wrong methods set out above, according to the LMS the correct way to do this manoeuvre is described thus: *'The complete train is drawn forward from the platform to a point beyond and clear of crossing 'A' and propelled to the Up platform. The engine is then detached and run round through crossings 'A' and 'B'. By adopting this method the Down line is cleared more expeditiously and the coaches are quickly at the Up platform in position for loading.'*

There is a fundamental lesson to be learnt form this example and it is all about line occupation. The LMS method clears the Down line quickly so that it can be made available for the passage of another train if required. Meanwhile, though the passenger train on the Up platform might have its engine at the wrong end, the stock is in the right place for any station work such as the of loading parcels and passengers prior to departure. The engine can run round at any time the other line is clear. The lesson from the LMS is, 'do not block running lines any longer than is necessary'.

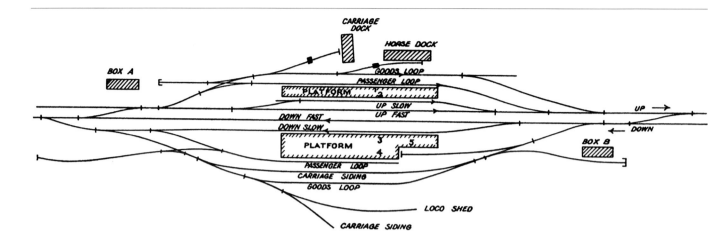

Above: **This plan was included in the LMS training manual in a section that dealt with exceptional traffic for carriage and horse docks. I have included it, not for that reason, but because it provides a useful plan for modellers who have the space to reproduce a major through station. The through lines do not serve any platforms, both express passenger and freight trains would run through on these Fast lines. In the Up direction platforms 1 and 2 are on loops. There are catch points at the rear of the line serving platform 2. Platform 1 is reached by the scissors crossover that also serves the short shunting line that ends by the buffer stop close to signal box A. There is a through goods loop in the Up direction, though when this was occupied by** anything other than a short train it would block the lines to the carriage and horse docks which can only be reached from this goods loop.

In the Down direction there is a loop that serves platform 3, but platforms 4 and 5 are both dead end bays. Working platform 5 is straightforward, Down trains run straight into the bay from the Down line and depart by the trailing crossover beyond signal box B, but platform 4 is not so easy. Unless there is a facing crossover not shown on the plan to the rear of signal box A in the Up direction, only Down trains could use platform 4. Another problem with both platforms 4 and 5 from an operating point of view is that neither has run round facilities. Unless the trains using these platforms were motor trains, then the engine would be trapped at the buffer stop end upon arrival.

On the Down side the drawing only shows a single line to the engine shed and carriage siding. This was not unusual with drawings of this nature, which concentrated upon running lines. In reality these facilities would be in keeping with the traffic requirements meaning in this instance that there would be many more lines relating to these features than those actually shown here. Finally on the Down side, note the siding that runs from the passenger loop and connects with the carriage siding and goods loop. It provides the catch point to protect the passenger lines at this end of the station.

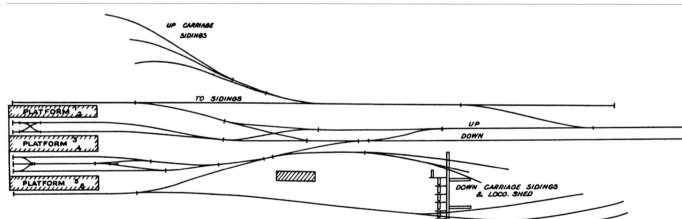

Above: **This illustrates what the LMS manual described as, 'certain phases of operation at a terminal station where the carriage sidings are situated in rear of the arrival platform'.** In this case, arriving trains can be disposed of by the train engine propelling coaches from platforms 4, 5 and 6 to the Down carriage sidings. Trains arriving at platforms 1, 2 and 3 can be disposed of by a shunting engine to the Up carriage sidings. From platform roads 4 and 5 the train engine can be released on arrival through the turn out road. From platform roads 2 and 3 the engine can be released through the unoccupied road. From platform roads 1 and 6 the train would have to be drawn from the platform by a shunting engine in order to release the train engine. Empty stock for trains starting here can be berthed by the train engines propelling from both the Up and Down carriage sidings either directly or by means of double shunting movements.

Once again the diagram is rather sparse when it comes to details of the track layout at the carriage sidings and the locomotive shed. However, the basic track plan in relation to the station throat, the terminal platforms and the arrangements for the disposal of coaching stock is a potentially useful blueprint for anyone thinking about modelling a large terminal station.

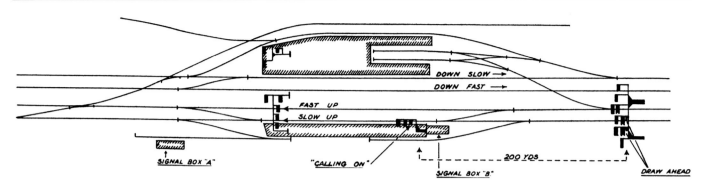

Above: **This example from the LMS manual illustrates the principles involved in circumstances of permissive block working which did apply at some passenger stations. Once again I quote from the LMS manual in full:** *'Diagram illustrating a through station where:*
1) The Up Slow Platform line is of sufficient length to hold one train only, worked under the Permissive Block Regulations (Station Yard Working), signalled so that when a train is leaving the platform a second train can follow
into the platform.

The second train has previously arrived at the home signal, having been accepted under Regulation 4 with road set to Bay line.

Having come to a stand, and the points having been reversed to lead to the Up platform line, the train is drawn up by means of the 'calling on' arm to the stop signal situated at Signal box 'B'.

The lever controlling the 'calling on' arm of this stop signal is then pulled off, and as the proceeding train moves off the

short track in advance of the signal, the 'calling on' arm automatically drops to permit the second train entering the platform, thus reducing the time lag to approximately one minute.

2) The Down platform line is signalled for dealing with trains starting in the Up direction.'

This method of working passenger trains, could easily be recreated on a model railway where it would arouse considerable interest.

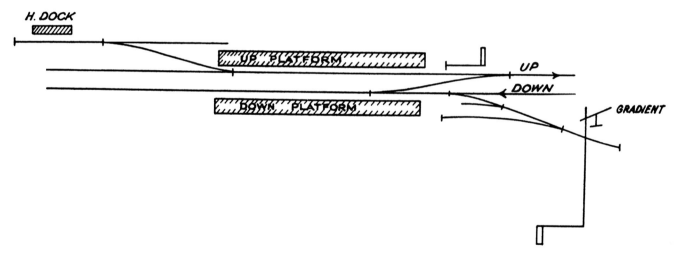

Above: **This is a simple through station with a horse dock on the Up side of the line and a siding on the Down side with the running lines connected by a single trailing crossover. This example was included in the LMS manual to show how to set back a passenger train into the horse dock siding to either detach or attach vehicles of a passenger train. Bear in mind that at the time the manual was drawn up, horse boxes were often conveyed in passenger trains. A few years ago in one of the magazines devoted to model railways there was an intense debate on the subject of shunting with passenger trains. As in other matters of this ilk, my response is always to refer to the rulebook.**

The LMS 1933 Rulebook is quite clear on the subject. Rule 116 states: *'(a) Vehicles must, whenever practicable, be attached to or detached from a passenger train without the train being moved.*
(b) When vehicles are being moved by an engine for the purpose of being attached to, or detached from, a passenger train, the brake pipes, where provided, must be connected so that the continuous brake maybe available during the operation.
(c) Before any vehicle containing passengers is moved over points, the person in charge of the operation must ascertain that the points are securely set, and that the line is clear and properly protected.'

Although I have quoted the LMS Rulebook, these procedures would be familiar to the other British railway companies. There is no question that a passenger train stopped at the Up platform would be allowed to set back to either detach or attach vehicles at the horse dock. In an ideal world, there would be a shunting engine on hand to do this, but setting a loaded passenger train back into the siding was certainly permissible under the rules.

Above: **Having looked at some station plans, let us now examine some actual stations layouts. Chilcompton station was on the S&DJR between Radstock and Shepton Mallet on a double track section of the line. The platforms were not of equal length, the one with the end and side loading dock with a loading gauge, was much shorter than the other. The siding leading from the dock ran parallel to the main line for some distance and was connected to both running lines by trailing points. In keeping with most stations of this nature, all the offices were on one side of the station. There was no footbridge, to get from one platform to the other, passengers had to walk over the barrow crossing, visible at the far end of the platforms. The large water tank supplied two water columns, one was at the far end of the platform, the other was on the opposite side of the line beyond where the photographer is standing.** J Moss

Left: **This undated picture of Yate station, which was located near Bristol on the MR line from Birmingham, was probably taken during the mid 1930s. Whilst there are many points of interest in the picture, the main reason for its inclusion is the wagon turntable on the Down side of the line. Yate would be classified as a country roadside station with limited goods facilities, but what a challenge for a modeller. Access to the goods yard was in the trailing direction only. An engine could set back into the goods shed, which was located just out of the picture to the left, from the Down line, or into the end loading dock, from the Up line. Access to any of the sidings required the use of the wagon turntable. As there is no capstan, wagons would have been moved by a shunting horse, or more likely by a man with a pinch bar. Note the revolving disc signals and the single blade trap points to protect the main line.**

Top right: **The simplest form of station was the unmanned halt, This is a view of Garston, on the Watford to St Albans branch, was taken in the BR era. The basic facilities at the halt consisted only of a simple corrugated iron waiting shelter on a wooden platform, two platform lights and a nameboard.** S Clennell

Centre right: **Gravelly Hill, on the ex-LNWR line between Birmingham and Lichfield, provides an example of a suburban passenger station without any goods facilities. Although not visible in this picture there was a waiting room on the right hand platform.**

Bottom: **I doubt if many would be tempted to build a model of a large provincial through station, but I have included this picture of the interior of Preston station, taken prior to the 1923 grouping, as an example of the work which would be involved. There is a wealth of complex detail in the ironwork of the pillars supporting the roof and on the footbridge. One of the unusual baffles that run over the lines is deflecting the faint exhaust from the L&Y tank engine. The parcels on the platform and on the trolleys have been placed there in readiness to be loaded into the next train at the platform.**

Left: **Some of the most interesting locations in Britain, from the modelling point of view, were those which hosted both steam and electric traction as may be observed from this 1966 picture taken at Birkenhead. Both types of traction brought their own clutter to the location. Electric trains required the third rail to supply them with power, this also created the need for warning notices such as that seen on the platform, Steam locomotives required water and from the parachute water tank in the picture, two locomotives could be supplied at once should the need arise. The brazier, which prevented the water from freezing in cold weather, was another essential piece of equipment which is sometimes overlooked by modellers.**

Below: **At first sight this train is on the wrong line but in fact it is a motor train, so the locomotive does not have to run round the coaches. The location is Tutbury, not far from my home in Staffordshire, and although we still have a railway and signal box the station no longer looks like this. The locomotive is one of the motor fitted BR standard 2-6-2 tanks, No 84006. The train worked over a now closed curve between the main line station at Burton-on-Trent and Tutbury and was known locally as 'The Tutbury Jenny'. This name is still perpetuated by a local pub and a walk along part of the former railway track bed, although it is now spelt as 'Jinny'. In this picture we can see some of the essential elements of a station with a level crossing, the footbridge for pedestrians, the wooden level crossing gates closing off the road and a wicket gates for pedestrians. As was normal, the road surface was level with the top of the rails. The signal box, another essential feature, is behind the photographer.** E Wood

Right: **Oakley station was on the London &
South Western Railway line between
Basingstoke and Salisbury. Like many
stations, at some point in its history, its
platforms were lengthened. When this
happened it was not uncommon for the old
and new parts of the platform to have two
different heights even though this must
have caused problems for passengers. This
charming wayside station has its signal box
on the platform and the sleepers of its
tracks buried in ballast. As no footbridge
was provided, passengers had to cross the
tracks using the barrow crossing.**

Centre right: **This is one of many places in
the book where a careful check is required
to ascertain whether the picture shows a
model or a real railway scene. Ambergate
was an unusual station with a triangular
layout. When I first saw this model I
thought it captured its atmosphere very
well. This picture of the EM gauge layout
confirms my original impression.** Tony
Wright

Below: **The four track layout through
Wellington station in Shropshire, on the
Shrewsbury to Wolverhampton line still
exists, though much else has changed. This
model captures the essence of the Western
Region in the early years of nationalisation
very well. The porter struggling with the
well loaded barrow on the platform ramp,
is a deft touch.** Tony Wright

Top: **In this delightful picture, a passenger train hauled by F6 class 2-4-2 tank No 67230, enters Monks Eleigh station. The model, to Scale 7 standards, represents an East Anglian branch during the early BR period. Some of the details add greatly to the realism of the layout, items such as the** signal wires, point rodding and the disc signal. Even the ballast has been carefully made to look not quite up to main line standards. Tony Wright

Above: **Ashburton, the erstwhile terminus of the now preserved Dart Valley branch, has** been modelled more than once. The GWR branch line is still one of the most popular subjects for modellers. Here a mixed train is seen departing from the station, however the make up of the train does not conform to the rules set out on page 80.
Courtesy Model Rail

PASSENGER TRAINS

The composition of the passenger trains which served the stations we have just discussed is a major and important topic. There were gradual changes to the composition and the nature of passenger trains over the decades and there is not the space here to identify all of these changes. Therefore, I have based the observations which follow, largely, but not entirely, on the post 1930 period.

When the railway companies were planning their timetables a number of factors contributed to the precise formation of trains. The timetable compilers began with the historical data based upon the number passengers expected to travel which obviously affected the composition of a train. Another factor was the time of day when a train ran or the distance it had to travel. These considerations dictated whether dining cars were required. These were usually included in special sets of coaches rostered to meet the requirements of a particular service. Sometimes dining cars did not stay with a set throughout its journey, they could be attached or detached en route. The modern railway does not like shunting and does not follow the practice of yesteryear whereby the composition of passenger trains could alter throughout the journey.

Many passenger trains in the age of steam did not present the tidy uniform appearance that, with the passing of time, perhaps some of us imagine we remember. Other factors took precedence. Operators were not interested in the look of their trains. What concerned them was that there was enough accommodation for each class of passenger and if that meant running brand new Third Class coaches next to a First Class vehicle which was 25 years old, so be it. Therefore it was not unusual to see different design styles of vehicles, or coaches from different eras, in the same formation.

Most passenger trains were made up of sets of coaches which ran more or less permanently coupled together. This was most obvious on the Southern Railway where these fixed formations were identified by having a set number painted on the vehicles at the outer ends of the sets. These formations were only interfered with if a carriage had to be withdrawn for urgent maintenance. In times of heavy traffic strengthening vehicles from a pool of unallocated coaches were added as required but were removed when not needed.

The use of fixed set formations was not restricted to express passenger services. Lesser formations were treated in the same way. An example of this was the LMS Western Division Inter-District three coach set that was made up of a Brake third, Composite and Brake Third. A two-coach formation would consist of a Brake Third and Composite, while a four coach set would have be two Brake Thirds with two Composites or one Composite and one Third.

The Brakes would be at the outer ends of the set, usually with the brake compartment at the far end. All the major British railway companies used similar set formations. A well known example of this was the GWR 'B' sets. These consisted of two Brake Composites. There was only only one First Class compartment in each coach, that in one vehicle was a smoker, the other was one non smoking.

The main limiting factors on the size of a passenger train were the power output of the locomotive, the nature of the road over which it was to run and the length of platforms en route. For example, an express passenger train hauled by a Class 5 4-6-0 locomotive between Birmingham and Derby, which was a fairly level road, could load up to 415 tons. However, over the gradients of the Settle & Carlisle line between Carlisle and Leeds, the same locomotive was only allowed to take 345 tons, a difference amounting to two corridor coaches.

Certain lines had also restrictions which applied to both locomotives and coaches. Those applying to locomotives are reasonably well known, restrictions to coaching stock are less so. One of these was the length of the platforms. For example, the short platforms at Fenchurch Street in London affected the length of the trains used on services to Shoeburyness and Southend. Narrow tunnels with restricted clearances, such as those on the Hastings line, dictated the use of stock that did not exceed a certain width. In other places longer carriages were not permitted to run over certain lines because of the danger of them fouling platforms on tight curves. This factor is rather relevant to model railways.

There were also usually restrictions concerning the conveyance of four wheeled nonpassenger carrying stock, such as milk tanks or horse boxes, and where they were to be marshalled in the train. Normally such vehicles were not allowed to form part of a train timed to run at speeds of over 60mph. Restrictions on the number of vehicles behind the rear brake van on certain lines was also imposed, due to heavy gradients on the line. Other brake vehicles, as far as possible were marshalled in the front of express trains. Each company had its own local restrictions either relating to types of stock or to sections of line. If one is basing a model on an actual location, it is as well to check what local strictures applied. Of course if one is creating a model of a fictitious location, the only regulations you need worry about are those which you impose yourself, though you should consider those which applied to similar lines elsewhere.

There were various classes of passenger trains. Expresses were the most important. Their composition could vary from perhaps as many as fifteen coaches including kitchen and dining cars to as few as two or three vehicles, still running under the express passenger train headcode. The latter would usually be one of the through coach sections of an express after it had been detached from the main train. The

working timetable set out what class of train each working was. It was this rather than the number of vehicles which determined the the status of each train.

What railway enthusiasts and modellers tend to refer to as local passenger or suburban passenger trains were known to railway staff as ordinary passenger trains. These were trains that generally, but not always, covered relatively short distances. Some of these, such as those travelling between Liverpool and Manchester, served major centres of population.

An ordinary passenger trains could be formed by a motor train. These were also known as auto trains, sometimes they were also called reversible trains or pull and push trains. The principle was the same and from the early 1900s many British railway companies used them. Only the description changed depending upon the company. They consisted of a locomotive, which pulled the train in one direction and pushed it in the other. When the engine was pushing the coaches the driver drove from a specially adapted compartment in the leading coach (see the illustration on page 35). The advantage these offered over conventional stock was that the locomotive did not have to run round at the end of a journey.

An important source of traffic for the steam railway was the excursion train. The first recorded excursion was organised by one Thomas Cook in the 1840s. It was only with the advent of widespread car ownership that such trains virtually ceased to run over the British railway system. The type of stock used varied immensely from modern open vestibule carriages to elderly stock now only used when required for excursion purposes. From the 1920s through to the BR period long distance excursion trains were made up from corridor and vestibule stock, often with a Dining Car. Short distance trains were marshalled by means of re-diagramming local train circuits or the use of elderly vehicles as described above.

Apart from workings which actually conveyed passengers, other types of trains ran under the regulations which governed the working of passenger trains. Parcels trains evolved as a response to increasing parcels traffic and the desire not to delay passenger trains, which previously had carried parcels in their brake carriage. Mail traffic could range from a single bag loaded at a country station to a complete train made up of purpose built sorting and stowage vans together with Travelling Post Offices, vehicles with the special apparatus designed to pick up and set down mailbags at speed.

Sometimes perishable goods traffic, products such as fish, meat, milk, fruit and flowers, was conveyed by passenger trains. This traffic might be accommodated in a single van or vans marshalled as part of a passenger train or could require a complete train of such vehicles, fully fitted with automatic brakes, running at express train speeds over long distances.

The carriage of certain types of goods and parcels on passenger trains in turn affected the work at station platforms. Even dedicated parcels trains en route to their destinations called at passenger stations and not goods depots to pick up and set down the merchandise they carried. This led to the common sight to of barrows loaded with parcels and mail on the station platforms. The station staff knew at what part of the platform the various vans on a particular working were likely to stop as they were usually marshalled in accordance with an agreed train order and thus would stop at the same place on the platform each day. The barrows containing the goods for the destinations served by those vans were able to be left at the the right place and the porters did not have to chase after the train before loading or unloading could take place.

A recurring theme in these pages is that modellers should seek inspiration and knowledge from the real railway. In keeping with this aim, it strikes me that the best way to understand something about how passenger train formations were organised, is to look at what was done on the prototype. The railway companies produced seasonal booklets detailing their train marshalling arrangements. These were for internal circulation only, but some have survived. The examples discussed on this page and that opposite are taken from the LMS Marshalling Arrangements which were effective from 9th July 1934. The cover of the booklet is reproduced, above right. The document is signed by the Chief Operating Officer. The reference urging staff to keep a look out for any shortage of room should bring a wry smile to many of today's travellers squeezed into two carriages for long cross country journeys. This information was then carefully recorded and would be used to prepare next year's timetable. Though these examples are from an LMS publication in my collection, it should be stressed that the other railway companies produced and circulated to their staff similar sets of marshalling instructions.

PASSENGER TRAIN
MARSHALLING ARRANGEMENTS
From JULY 9th, 1934, until further notice.

CLASS "A" STOCK.—TRAINS SHOWN UNDER THIS HEADING MUST BE FORMED OF STOCK STENCILLED "A" ON THE RIGHT-HAND SIDE OF THE TONNAGE PLATE ON THE END OF EACH VEHICLE. RESTAURANT CARS AND SLEEPING CARS ARE NOT SO MARKED, BUT ARE TREATED AS CLASS "A" STOCK.

Passenger Trains must be made up strictly in accordance with the arrangements shown herein, and must not be altered without authority from the Divisional Superintendent of Operation.
The loading of the trains must be closely watched and any daily shortage of room, light loading, or deviation from the scheduled marshalling, immediately reported.

Where Brake Carriages are shown in this Marshalling Book next to the Engine, they must, as far as practicable, be run with the Brake compartment in front. When changing this type of vehicle owing to stoppage for repairs or other causes, Marshalling Inspectors, Foremen and Shunters must see that the vehicle to be substituted has the Brake compartment at the leading end, taking steps to have it turned if necessary.

TONNAGE LOADING.

No Train must be made up to more than 500 tons, and not more than 15 Bogie Vehicles may be run on any train, except where laid down herein, or specially authorised by the Divisional Superintendent of Operation.

EXPLANATION OF REFERENCES.

§ Steel Vehicles.	† Four or Six Wheeled Stock.
‡ Empty Trains.	**NC** Non Corridor.
M Mondays excepted.	**MO** Mondays only.
MS Mondays and Saturdays excepted.	**MSO** Mondays and Saturdays only, etc.
	A Class "A" Stock.

Derby.

C. R. BYROM,
Chief Operating Manager.

Opposite page, first column, top: **The first train to come under our scrutiny is the 6.25pm St Pancras – Manchester Central. This is a rather interesting example of a train where the composition varies during the week and vehicles are both attached and detached during the journey. The Third Class coach from circuit 1049c, after arriving from St Pancras, is sent to Liverpool on the 7.10am from Manchester, returning to Manchester that afternoon. This is an example of a through coach working from St Pancras to Matlock and Buxton. The vehicles are detached and then attached to the rear of a train from Derby.**

Opposite page, first column, bottom: **The 5.0pm Bristol – Sheffield and Bradford is another example of a train whose** composition varies from day to day and during the course of the journey. The tonnage is greater on a Saturday and the the train's composition is altered at Birmingham, Derby and Sheffield. For example, the Saturdays only train was strengthened by the addition of a Third Class coach that was worked through and another Third that was added at Sheffield. It would add great interest to the operation of a model railway set along the route of a train like this, if as part of the operating sequence, coaches were attached or detached. Whilst many layouts run to a timetable of events, I cannot recall seeing an example where the operators make a distinction between the various days of the week. A glance at any historic railway timetable will reveal that there were many daily variations.

Opposite page, middle column, top: **The 8.25pm St Pancras – Derby was a train which conveyed another company's vehicle in an LMS formation, in this case a LNER Passenger Brake Van. This train includes a total of four brake vans as well as a non - corridor tail comprising six vehicles.**

Opposite page, middle column, lower: **The 2.45pm Carlisle – St Pancras was an Anglo Scottish train which combined Glasgow and Edinburgh portions at Carlisle and then had additional vehicles attached at Leeds for the rest of the journey on to London. The Edinburgh portion consisted of a LNER Third Brake and Composite Brake while the Glasgow portion included two coaches, a Third and a Brake Composite that are detached at Leeds and are worked forward to Manchester Victoria.**

Marshalling.		Circuit No.
6.25 p.m. ST. PANCRAS—MANCHESTER (Cen.).		
Class " A " Stock.		
bThird (MFSO)	—Manchester (Cen.)	1049c
Third (SO)	— Do.	1244b
§Third Brake (24)	— Do.	66
Third	⎱	
Third Vestibule (56)	⎰	
Third Vestibule (42)	Do.	66
Kitchen Car	⎱	
First Vestibule (42)	⎰	
First Brake (27)	⎰	
cCompo.Brake (9-21)	⎰ Matlock & Buxton	77
		77a
fThird (42)	—Derby	1050a
d§5 Brake Van (S)	— Do.	—
Attach rear Leicester (S):—		
e§†Brake Van	—Derby	—

Tonnage—285 (315 MFO, 330 SO) St. Pancras.
300 (335 MFO, 330 SO) Leicester.
210 (240 MFO, 270 SO) Derby.

b Sent Liverpool on 7.10 a.m. from Manchester, and returns 4.55 p.m.

c Transferred Derby to rear of 9.5 (S), 9.16 p.m. (SO) to Buxton.

d Returns 3.32 p.m.

e Received on 12.35 a.m. from Leeds. Returns 7.26 p.m. (S), 7.29 p.m. (SO).

f Received 1.58 p.m. from Derby (SO).

Marshalling.		Circuit No.
5.0 p.m. BRISTOL—SHEFFIELD AND BRADFORD.		
bThird (MF)	⎰ Sheffield (for Bradford)	1254d
Third (SO)	— Do.	7 40 a.m.
A§Third Brake (24)	⎱	
AThird (42)	Do.	118
AThird Vestibule (42)	⎰	
First Brake (27)	⎰	
Third (FO)	— Do.	1254c
cBrake Van	—Leeds	—
Third (SO)	—Sheffield	1254d
First R. Car (24)	⎱ Derby	163
AThird Vestibule (42)	⎰	
Attach front Birmingham:—		
Third (S)	—Derby	1189
Third (ThO)	— Do.	1190
Attach front Sheffield (off 6.15 p.m. ex St. Pancras) (Saturdays excepted):—		
Compo. Brake (12-18)	⎱	
First R. Car (24)	⎰ St. Pancras Bradford	39
Third Vestibule (42)	⎰	
Third Brake (18)	⎰	

Tonnage—245 (215 MO, 305 SO) Bristol.
275 (245 MO, 305 ThO, 305 SO) Birmingham.
170 (140 MO, 230 SO) Derby.
230 (310 FO, 175 SO) Sheffield.

b Sent Bradford 10.4 p.m. (S), 10.16 p.m. (SO) from Sheffield.

c Return 2.55 a.m.

		Circuit No.
8.25 p.m. ST. PANCRAS—DERBY.		
§Third Brake (40)	⎱	
Compo. (18-32)	⎰	
AThird (42)	Derby.	37
Compo. (18-32)	⎰	
§Third Brake (40)	⎰	
bBrake Van	—Newcastle	—
bBrake Van (S) (LNE)	— Do.	—
bBrake Van	—Hull	—
cBrake Van	—Bradford	—
dThird (SO)	—Leicester	—
NC Third (FS)	—Bedford	1005
NC Third (FO)	— Do.	1033
NC Compo.	— Do.	1063
NC Third (SO)	— Do.	1001
eNC Third (SO)	— Do.	1570
eNC Third (SO)	— Do.	1570
Attach front Leicester (S):—		
fRest Car (24)	⎱ Derby	38
fThird Vestibule (42)	⎰	

Marshalling.		Circuit No.
2.45 p.m. (S) CARLISLE—ST. PANCRAS.		
(12.10 p.m. from Edinburgh, Waverley.)		
(12.10 p.m. from Glasgow, St. Enoch.)		
(Reversed at Leeds.)		
Class " A " Stock.		
Third Brake (32) (LNE)	⎱	
Compo. Brake (12-24) (LNE)	Edinburgh St. Pancras	10
§Third Brake (24)	⎰	
Third Vestibule (42)	⎰	
Third Vestibule (42)	⎰	
Kitchen Car	Glasgow do.	8
First Vestibule Corr. (18-12)	⎰	
First Brake (27)	⎰	
cThird	—Glasgow Manchester (Vic.)	—
cCompo. Brake (9-21) —	Do. do.	137
Attach front Leeds:—		
dCompo. (MO)	⎰ Bradford St. Pancras	1299a

		Circuit No.
6.15 p.m. (S) ST. PANCRAS—BRADFORD.		
(Divided at Chesterfield.)		
Class " A " Stock.		
bCompo. Brake (12-32)	⎱ Bradford	47
bThird Vestibule (42)	Do.	164
bFirst R. Car (18)	⎰	
bThird Brake (24)	— Do.	50
cdCompo. Brake (12-32)	⎱ Halifax	48
ceCompo. Brake (12-32)	⎰	
ceFirst R. Car (24)	⎱ Sheffield (for Bradford)	39
ce ThirdVestibule (42)	⎰	
ceThird Brake (24)	⎰	

Tonnage—290 St. Pancras.
130 Chesterfield.

b Form 9.3 p.m. Chesterfield to Leeds via Eckington.
c Form 9.13 p.m. Chesterfield to Sheffield.
d Transferred Sheffield to 9.36 p.m. to Thornhill.
e Transferred to 9.45 p.m. Sheffield to Leeds (5.0 p.m. from Bristol).

Marshalling.		Circuit No.
5.32 p.m. (S.) ST. PANCRAS—NOTTINGHAM.		
§Third Brake (40)	⎱	
Compo. (18-32)	⎰	
AThird (42)	Nottingham	36
Compo. (18-32)	⎰	
§Third Brake (40)	⎰	
bRest. Car (24)	⎱ Leicester	38
bThird Vestibule (42)	⎰	

Tonnage—210 St. Pancras.
150 Leicester.

b Sent Derby 11.8 p.m. from Leicester.

The train reverses at Leeds, as that is a terminal station, which means that the Composite, attached on Mondays only from Bradford to St Pancras, will now be at the front of the train.

This page, right hand column, top: The 6.15pm St Pancras – Bradford is a further example of a train that both attaches and detaches vehicles en route. Note the coupling of the First Restaurant Car with the Third Vestibule catering for 18 First Class and 42 Third Class passengers. This working provides a good example of how the composition of an express train could be altered during its journey. Chesterfield comes into the category of a large provincial station and it is not an unrealistic prototype for a model. There are many similar locations throughout the British railway system which could also be tackled and would provide great operating interest and challenges.

This page, right hand column, bottom: Compared with some of the other examples which we have been looking at, the 5.32pm St Pancras – Nottingham train is a fairly straightforward working. However, note that the Restaurant Car and Third Vestibule are detached at Leicester and later worked through to Derby, out of service.

The study of documents like this Train Marshalling Arrangements booklet or old working timetables, is quite fascinating and opens a window onto the complexity of train workings in past decades. In looking at such material one also achieves a great insight into how the railways were operated all those years ago. It would be of course incorrect to imagine that all express passenger trains circuits were altered in this way of some of the examples given here. Most workings went from A to B without such complexities along the way.

Left: **Through coaches on the real thing. At Ballinluig, where the branch to Aberfeldy joined the main line from Perth to Inverness, on the 6th September 1952, ex-Caledonian 4-4-0 No 54502, has been uncoupled from its south bound main line working to pick up a through carriage from Aberfeldy to Perth which had been brought to this junction station by the branch line service.** N R Knight

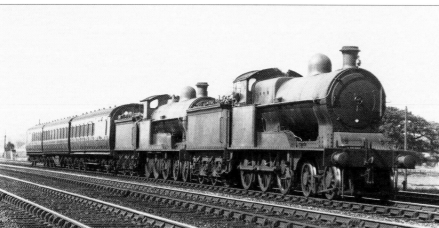

Centre left: **The locomotive headlamp code confirms this is an ordinary passenger train made up of three coaches with the brake compartments at the ends of the train in accordance the instructions in the LMS marshalling book. The use of two large ex-LNWR 4-6-0s on such a short train calls for an explanation. The leading engine was probably coupled up to the train engine to avoid it having to run later as a light engine working. This was sometimes referred to as, 'saving a block;' a means of reducing line occupation. It looks good when reproduced on a model.**

Below: **It was the seating capacity that was important, not the age of the coaches as this GWR service at Torquay illustrates. The train is hauled by 45XX class 2-6-2T No 4553. This view also provides a good example of the value of trap points. If those wagons on the centre road ran forward for any reason, they could foul the platform line, had there not been a trap point to derail them before they could come into contact with a train on the platform line.**

Right: **This ex-LNWR pull and push train was photographed at Kenilworth in 1938. The Driving trailer is a composite, with four First and two Third Class compartments. The coaches beyond the engine are similar to these. The LMS used ex-LNWR 0-6-2 and 2-4-2 tanks for this work on the Western Division. The locomotive in this instance is 2-4-2T, No 6653, sandwiched between the coaches. Although it was more usual to have the engine at one end of the train, it was not uncommon to have a locomotive in the middle of a set of four coaches.**
H J Stretton Ward

Centre right: **Cattle wagons or horse boxes were often found on passenger trains, especially on branch lines. This was acceptable practice providing the vehicle was fitted with oil axleboxes and equipped with either through pipes or the automatic vacuum brake. It was usual to attach the vehicle next to the engine, as shown here in this 1934 picture of a passenger train, hauled by ex-LNWR 2-4-0 No 25001.**
G Coltas

Below: **It was not unusual for the locomotive of one company to haul the stock of another, in particular when the line was jointly owned. This picture shows an unidentified LNWR 0-6-0 Cauliflower 0-6-0 on the Birkenhead Joint line in 1919, hauling a train of GWR coaches headed by two GWR Syphons, vehicles which were often used to carry milk in churns,**

Top: **Express trains could vary in length. This July 1950 view of the 6.45pm Down St Pancras to Leicester express, hauled by ex-LMS Jubilee 4-6-0 No 45607, consists of a passenger brake van and seven ex-LMS Stanier coaches. An express train of this size could be accommodated on many model railway layouts.** E D Bruton

Above: **All trains carried a headlamp code to show signalmen what type of working the train was. However, more than one type of traffic was conveyed under the class C headlamp code, seen on this parcels working headed by one of the Caprotti fitted Class 5 4-6-0s No 44754, approaching Dore & Totley in June 1954. In addition to** parcels trains, this classification included **trains conveying fish, fruit, livestock, pigeons, general perishable traffic and empty coaching stock workings. There was only one headcode for all of these but three signal box bell codes were used to offer more specific identification to this class of working.** E D Bruton

Below: **Class 5 4-6-0 No M4820 was photographed in August 1948 when the locomotive was working a Down train of empty milk tanks. The single van behind the tender is for churn traffic. A passenger brake van with four more tanks behind it makes up the rear of the train. It is a** common misconception that the usual practice was to put the brake van at the end of a train like this. If the train was marshalled in the order seen here, the guard would have a more comfortable ride.
E D Bruton

Bottom: **The intense steam suburban services which were once a feature of the London main line terminal stations are represented by this picture of 0-6-2T No 4734 at the head of a train of close coupled articulated stock leaving Kings Cross with a New Barnet train.**

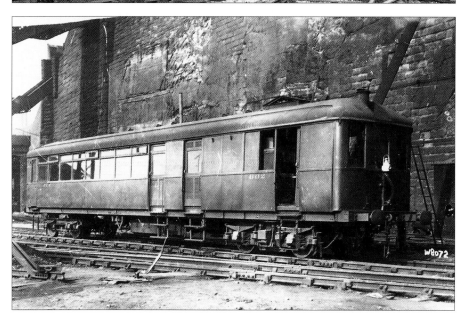

Above: **Modellers need not be too concerned about running passenger trains with locomotives working tender first. This practice was not uncommon on the prototype as is demonstrated by this undated view of LNER 4-4-0 No 2139 at Immingham Dock on a three coach passenger train.**

Centre left: **This picture is not quite what it may seem at first glance but it offers another operational option which could add interest to a model. This picture, taken at Manchester London Road in March 1953, shows ex-GCR 4-4-2T No 67421 working the 5.17pm Manchester London Road to Glossop motor train. The two coach push pull set has been strengthened by the addition of an ordinary non-corridor coach. This is clearly not a Driving trailer so for the return journey, this carriage will have to be shunted to the other end of the train. This formation is perfectly acceptable and within the rules even though it may look a bit odd.**

Left: **As well as using push pull trains, in their search for other economical methods to work lightly used lines, the British railway companies experimented with self propelled vehicles. The LNER employed with reasonable success a number of these Sentinel steam railcars. No 602, one of four railcars Nos 600 - 603, that were added to the joint stock of the Cheshire Lines Committee, is seen here at Brunswick in Liverpool.**

Left: **Light railways have their own particular attraction for modellers usually because the rolling stock is of considerable vintage or as unusual as this vehicle used on the Kelvedon & Tollesbury line in Essex. This open coach with verandas, proudly bearing its new British Railways number, E60461, is more like the sort of vehicle that might be seen on an Irish narrow gauge line than on a standard gauge branch in Britain.** J H Aston

Below: **Often due to lack of space, it is difficult for modellers to successfully recreate the lengthy steam hauled express trains which are so evocative to my generation. I think that the Stoke Summit layout has captured the flavour of a main line remarkably well. This picture shows what can be done by a group of dedicated modellers as they seek to show what a main line was like during the steam era.** Tony Wright

Left: **This picture of the Biggleswade layout gives an air of space, the express passenger train passing a freight train was commonplace in the steam era.** Tony Wright

MOVING THE GOODS

Earlier we looked at some of the industries which provided much of the goods traffic for the railways of Britain. Here, we will first explore some of the broad principles which were involved in moving large volumes of goods traffic, the core business of the steam railway. Later, we will examine the formation of the freight trains that were used to move the various classes of traffic that ran over the British railway system.

The movement of all freight traffic can be divided into three separate, but related functions, loading at the originating point, marshalling the loaded traffic into trains and unloading at the terminating point. While the first and third functions would, as far as individual consignments are concerned, be carried out at a specific place, shunting could enter the equation at many points along the way.

Traffic, of one sort or another, flowed in all directions and a loading point for one source of traffic could become an unloading point for traffic travelling in the opposite direction. For example, the principal traffic carried by British railways during the period covered by this book was coal. This of course originated at the collieries where it was loaded into empty wagons. The colliery was thus the originating point for loaded wagons and a receiving point for empty wagons. To give another example, wagons carried all manner of goods to the docks for export. When the goods had been unloaded the same vehicles, now empty, were used to carry imported goods to their inland destinations, or in railway terms, the receiving point.

Under the general heading of originating and receiving points were a vast array of places where wagons, either loaded or unloaded could be received. These included goods stations and depots, warehouses and private sidings, docks, wharves, gas and electricity generating plants and collieries. One of the most important of these was the goods station and this came in a variety of shapes and sizes.

A small goods station usually consisted of a building with only one floor, served by a single road accommodating a few wagons at any one time. Such sheds had fairly wide decks, designed to ensure adequate space to deal with traffic going in both directions, outgoing traffic that would be loaded into rail wagons and incoming traffic perhaps being loaded onto road vehicles for the last leg of its journey. Space was also needed at a goods depot to store traffic awaiting movement. The number of sidings in the yard varied depending upon the amount and type of traffic that was dealt with at that location.

Medium size goods stations often had sheds with more than one floor in order to provide more space for storage purposes. They might also have side and end loading docks. The yard facilities would also be larger and could include sidings for local coal merchants, together with others dealing with livestock and any traffic that was local in nature. This could be fruit and vegetables or items manufactured locally.

A goods station's geographical location would set the traffic pattern. For example not all the coal traffic might be for domestic users. The demands of a local industry could increase the amount of coal being dealt with and the number of coal merchants using the facility would depend upon the size and nature of the community the station served. There might be only one merchant renting siding space or there could be several. If it was a cattle producing area, a large cattle dock might be required. In other places, a dock able to accommodate a single cattle wagon would suffice. Therefore it is difficult to generalise; modellers should find suitable prototypes and model accordingly.

The largest goods stations were to be found at the principal centres of population. All the major cities had extensive goods sheds and warehouses. Even after the grouping, in places like Birmingham and Manchester which were served by more than one of the Big Four companies, each concern had its own yards and warehouses. By their very size, city goods stations are very difficult to model convincingly. I speak from experience here, as I had intended to include a town goods station on my own Dewsbury layout. The original version of this was abandoned because I did not feel it was big enough to capture the atmosphere that I sought. The second version, which at the time of writing is complete as far as the track is concerned, is large for a model, but of modest size when compared to a the size of goods station that a place like Dewsbury would have warranted in reality.

In addition to the goods sheds and warehouses there should be facilities for handling domestic coal and coke, livestock and there should be side and end docks to enable road vehicles to be moved onto or from rail vehicles. Not all traffic was handled within the goods shed, large bulky items such as timber was also dealt with at many goods stations. These would have been were handled in the open yard so suitable crane power would be required. Cart roads to provide access to the sidings where loading or unloading was carried out are necessary and we must not forget such buildings as weigh bridges, stables for the railway horses, store huts and staff rooms.

Another important source and destination for goods traffic was the private siding. These sidings were lines that were connected to the main line railways but did not form part of them. It was the usual practice to have a gate across the point where the railway company's property ended. Individual agreements between a siding's owner and the railway company determined if the railway company's engines were allowed onto the private lines. If the private owner had his own locomotives then it was less likely that the railway company, which would have charged for the work, would have done any shunting on these lines.

Some private sidings were small railways in their own right, with locomotives, internal user wagons and a number of staff, while others were no more than a single siding that was connected to the railway. These single or two siding affairs were usually shunted by the railway company when the local trip working came to deliver or collect wagons. Depending upon the traffic flow, this could be once or twice a day or rather less frequently. The advantage of a private siding, where the works were rail connected, was that there was an immense saving in not having to cart all the inward or outward traffic to and from the nearest goods station.

A lot of goods traffic originated at docks, wharves and canals. Some of these were owned by the railway companies, others were privately owned. Where another mode of transport was involved transshipment of goods from one to the other was inevitable. Though this was inherently costly it would take place if there was an economic imperative to do so. One example of this was the movement of coal that came by sea from the north east coalfield to southern ports where it was transhipped to rail for a short distance to its final destination. In other words the coal went by rail, sea and finally rail because it was cheaper than sending the coal the entire distance by rail.

The vast bulk of the goods traffic in Britain either came from or went to the major centres of population and was handled at the large city goods stations. Trains ran on certain days at fixed times between these centres. Each train would usually include wagons for several destinations. As loading took place in the goods station the wagons that conveyed traffic for specific destinations would be clearly marked for the benefit of the loading gangs. If it was found that there was not enough traffic bound for one location to fill a wagon, those goods would be combined with consignments for other nearby destinations and sorted again en route.

Although most modellers do not have the space or inclination to build large marshalling yards they do construct goods stations, which as we have noted above, came in a variety of shapes and sizes. Most of the larger goods stations had sidings where wagons for outgoing trains were marshalled. It was also necessary for incoming trains to be marshalled so that the vehicles were unloaded in order of priority and placed in the correct part of the goods station prior to being unloaded. For example a train that contained wagons of fruit and vegetables that were to go to the local market for sale that day would be unloaded before non perishable goods that could be delivered by the railway company when the carter made his rounds.

Because marshalling sidings took up a lot of space, which was at a premium in the urban areas where the goods stations were located, the railway companies usually built their great marshalling yards out in the open countryside where land was cheaper than in urban areas. Perhaps I should qualify this by saying that over the years in some places, the towns caught catch up with the countryside where these yards were located. A good example of this was at Small Heath in Birmingham where Bordesley Sidings when originally opened were bounded by open fields. When I knew it as a working marshalling yard, it was surrounded by streets and houses.

There are several essential elements to a marshalling yard. The first was the arrival or reception sidings where incoming trains were placed. Here a train would be examined. Some wagons would be marked in chalk to indicate to the shunter where in the yard they were to be placed. In the departure sidings, wagons would be shunted to form outgoing trains. Shunting necks were also required to allow the shunting engine to break up incoming and make up the outgoing trains. Stowage sidings for surplus wagons, stored prior to being worked away and cripple sidings for wagons that were not fit to travel further, due to either a defect on the wagon or the load, which may have become displaced, were also essential elements of the complex.

Related to the large marshalling yards, in that they played an important part in moving traffic around the country, were the exchange sidings. Whereas marshalling yards normally dealt with the traffic of one company, at exchange sidings, traffic was transferred from one company to another. After the grouping in 1923 some of these exchanges were between different divisions of the same company

For example in Birmingham there was the appropriately named Exchange Sidings, where the London & North Western and the Midland companies exchanged wagons. After 1923 the exchanges continued but were now between the Western and Midland divisions of the LMS. The principle of exchanging traffic did not cease after nationalisation. From a modelling standpoint there is much to be said for a layout based upon exchange traffic. Usually there were a few sidings, probably double ended, with one or maybe two shunting necks. The similarity with a marshalling yard was that both required a shunting line from which the wagons could be propelled into a fan of sorting sidings. For modellers a consideration might be that whereas at a marshalling yard one would normally only see the the locomotives of just the one company, in this respect exchange sidings offered more variety. Here the locomotives and brake vans of more than one company could be seen.

There are many points of interest in this picture of the South Eastern & Chatham Railways goods station at Stewarts Lane in London. Although few modellers would even attempt to build this type of station there are many aspects that apply to the smaller depots that are reproduced. One feature which was common to many places was the use of stone setts to form the roadway. These are laid here in an irregular manner. The setts and the hard standing came up to rail level. There were thus no sleeper ends to trip over and certainly no ballast to be seen. There was plenty of room between the sidings to enable the carts to be backed up to or alongside the rail vehicles for loading or unloading purposes. The merchandise was packed in a variety of boxes, crates, bales and barrels. Goods were often sheeted over to protect them from the weather. In this view, apart from the steam lorry in the foreground, all other road transport that can be seen, is horse drawn. The by-products of this form of traction, a large pile of which can be seen in the foreground, had to be taken away by rail, though oddly this is something which is rarely modelled!

Above: **This is a wonderfully atmospheric view of a small Midland Railway goods yard taken in the early years of the last century. Its location has unfortunately not been established. The usual way in which modellers portray the handling of local coal traffic is to have a siding where the** coal merchants wagons stand, beside which is an enclosed area which holds the coal after it has been taken from the rail wagon. This photograph depicts what actually happened. The coal is being bagged within the rail wagon and then transferred to a horse drawn vehicle. A wooden platform to assist loading by propping up a wagon door, can also be seen. Coal sidings were often arranged in pairs with road access from one side of the rail vehicle only. There was also room between the sidings to stack the coal and to allow access to road vehicles.

Above: **Frizinghall is between Shipley and Bradford and this 1950s view is typical of the rather run down appearance of parts of the British railway system at this time. This is an interesting layout which has promise for the modeller. Frizinghall was a large suburban station with quite an extensive goods yard, seen here to the right of the** picture. The passenger lines run through the station and are separated from the goods lines, those nearest to the camera, by a wall. It was the normal practice to fence off any goods line if it ran alongside a passenger platform. There was a private siding at Frizinghall which served the mill, seen at the far right of the picture. The yard is being shunted by an unidentified Class 4F 0-6-0. Whilst the locomotive is engaged on these duties, the rest of its train has been left standing on the siding next to the Down goods line. R S Carpenter collection

Right: **Although photographed towards the end of its active life, this 1961 picture of the goods shed at Uppingham has been included to show a typical wooden built goods shed at a small country station. The essential features of this type of goods shed are, a siding for the vehicle that is to be either loaded or unloaded, a deck where a road vehicle can be placed and office accommodation. All these can be seen in this picture. The covered goods van is alongside the loading deck, which could accommodate about three vehicles. Road vehicles used the other side of the goods shed. The goods being transhipped were moved across the deck of the goods shed under cover. It was not always normal practice to have an awning on both sides of the goods shed. The office accommodation here was provided in the wooden hut at the end of the shed nearest the camera.**
  A G Ellis collection

Below: **The brewery railways in Burton-on-Trent were considerable to say the least. Sadly they are no more but a model of the system at the Bass Museum there, gives visitors a good idea of the extent of the system. This picture, taken in September 1934, shows Allsop's Brewery No.8 at** **Brook Street Burton. The sharp curves, like the one seen here, which abounded on the system, made large buffer heads essential. Compare the size of the buffers on the locomotive and those on the wagon.** M F Yarwood

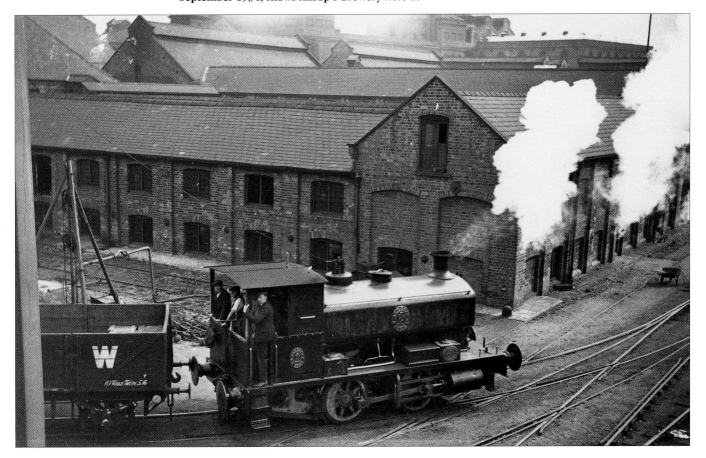

GOODS TRAINS

I could probably devote this entire book to the subject of goods and mineral trains before I exhausted everything that could be said, so of necessity, this can only be a brief overview of the subject.

During the early years of our railway history the classification of both passenger and goods trains was, compared with the British Railways period, fairly straight-forward. During the nineteenth century, Working Timetables would categorise freight trains as goods, cattle, empties or coal. The term express goods was also used to a limited degree. As with so much on the steam railway, once a way of conducting the business was established and found to be effective, there was little change in the methods used over the year. Nor did the classification of the traffic change very much.

There are really two types of train, those working mineral traffic and the rest. The latter, which conveyed goods traffic, were subdivided into trains that travelled between major centres and those which were more local.

In the final years of steam traction, the most important freights were identified as Class C workings. These trains were fully fitted and could be given the road to run in front of ordinary passenger trains. Some trains within this category were composed entirely of coaching stock vehicles. If a train was made up of freight stock these had to have brake pipes fitted throughout the train, and the automatic brake had to be operative on not less than half the wagons for the train to fit into this classification. Class C trains usually ran between major centres, but it was not unusual for these trains

Opposite page, top: **The traffic lurking unseen within the vans in this picture is still an important one for Britain's railways. The photograph was taken in the mid 1920s at Coventry. The locomotive is owned by the Daimler company and it is posed at the head of a train of vans which are labelled as containing, Daimler Show Cars. The diverse collection of vans in which the car are being transported share a common feature, in that they all have end opening doors to enable the cars to be driven onto them. The privately owned locomotive is here on railway company tracks, this was something that could be permitted under local arrangements.** NRM Derby Collection DY 14114

Opposite page, bottom: **The old L&NWR branch to Oxford terminated at Rewley Road station in the city. Here, as at so many locations, in particular at the end of branch lines, the goods station and passenger stations were side by side.**

to make at least one stop for examination where some wagons could be detached and others added to the train. A Class D train was similar to the Class C, except that the automatic brake was required to be operative on one third of its vehicles. Class D trains ran slightly slower than Class C workings because of the reduced braking power available to the driver.

An example of this class of train was the 4.00am from Water Orton, near Birmingham, to Carlisle. This was an important fitted express freight train. It stopped en route for water and examination but the train was not booked to attach or detach. The make up of the train at Water Orton was described, using terms which railwaymen would understand, but which might appear somewhat mysterious to the uninitiated, as; College fitted, Caledonian fitted, NB fitted, Carlisle proper and exchange not fitted. Most of the wagons that left Water Orton were being worked forward to destinations beyond Carlisle. College goods station is in Glasgow while NB was shorthand for the old North British Railway and referred to traffic bound for Edinburgh. The train was limited to 39 wagons when worked by a Class 4F 0-6-0 or 45 wagons when worked by a 2-6-0 Horwich Mogul or a Class 5 or 5X 4-6-0 passenger engine. The distance it had to travel was about 226 miles and it was one of the longest through runs made by a goods train on a regular basis.

The official documents relating to the Water Orton to Carlisle goods confirm that a passenger engine could work the train. The use of passenger engines on the principal express freight trains was not uncommon prior to the increased availability of 4-6-0 mixed traffic engines in the 1930s. They also stipulate that wagons were to be marshalled in a specific order to assist the shunters when the train arrived at Carlisle. This class of goods train provided a service that connected with other fast goods trains and they enabled traffic to travel long distances in a comparatively short period of time. As evidence of the slow pace of change on the steam railway, it is worth noting that even after 1948, references to companies like the Caledonian and the North British, were still in regular use even though these companies had ceased to exist in 1923.

Another type of train, still within the express freight train category, was the 'Maltese', so called because it was distinguished in the working timetable by a Maltese cross. This meant that the train was to run with at least four wagons that were fitted with an automatic brake coupled to the engine. Although these wagons provided some additional braking power, this type of train was not booked to travel as fast as Class C or D.

An example of a Maltese was the 4.40pm from Water Orton marshalling yard to Crewe. This included the four fitted vehicles at the head of the train, followed by traffic for Manchester London Road. Next came wagons for Manchester Liverpool Road and finally traffic

for what was described as, Bushbury exchange. The classification book said that the exchange traffic could include, fruit traffic for the NS line (North Staffordshire section) and traffic for Huddersfield. At Bushbury sidings, in Wolverhampton, the four fitted wagons for Crewe plus any other Crewe traffic remained coupled to the engine. The rest of the train which had been brought from Water Orton was detached and other wagons which had been collected at Bushbury destined for Crewe were added before the train went forward.

The final type of express freight train was the Class F on which no additional braking power was provided by the wagons. This class of train could both run over considerable distances or be little more than a local working. The working I have chosen to highlight was one that ran over what was really no more than a branch line. As many modellers focus on lines such as those used by this train, I hope they will find this example, the 3.10am express freight from Bedford to Stratford-on-Avon, of interest. The train, starting behind the engine, was to be composed of wagons for Towcester and exchange, Evesham, Ashchurch, Cheltenham, Gloucester proper and Gloucester and exchange. The instructions were that upon arrival at Olney wagons should be attached in marshalled order. This meant that any traffic for Ashchurch was to be put with the other wagons for that destination and traffic to be exchanged at Gloucester was to be placed accordingly. At Towester wagons could be detached for the Banbury line or for Blisworth. At Stratford the train terminated and the wagons that were going south were attached to a through freight train from Stratford to Gloucester that stopped at Ashchurch and Cheltenham. This type of working demonstrates how over the years an interconnecting system of freight trains evolved which ran throughout the country enabling merchandise to be conveyed from anywhere to everywhere throughout Britain.

The final type of through freight train was the Class H. I have chosen an example that I used to work when I was in the Evesham link at Saltley. This was the 6.00pm through freight from Beckford, near Ashchurch, to Birmingham Lawley Street. This working often conveyed fruit and vegetables from the many producers in the Vale of Evesham, the exact mix depended upon the season. The train was booked to convey traffic for Evesham and beyond. At Evesham we were to detach any wagons from Beckford that were to go to stations on the former Great Western system and attach additional traffic from Evesham. This traffic was classified as either bound for Camp Hill, where traffic for the Birmingham area was concentrated, or Lawley Street and Exchange. Lawley Street dispatched trains to stations on the Midland Division, Exchange Sidings served stations on the Western Division of the LMS.

We booked on and went to Evesham by passenger train where we relieved the Evesham men who were looking after our locomotive.

This 1952 view, taken at Standish Junction near Gloucester, shows a good trains hauled by ex-LMS 2-6-0 No 42815, running under Class C headlamps. A variety of types of train could come under this classification, here we have a livestock train, which is piped throughout, with the automatic brake operative on at least half the vehicles in the train.

We ran engine and brake van, (propelling the van) to Beckford were we picked up the first part of the train. At slack times this could consist of only a single van. At Evesham we stood in the station platform while the train was made up, some traffic being attached by the Western Region shunting engine that came behind us via the slip road from the former Great Western station. We departed with any Camp Hill traffic 'on the engine' followed by the Lawley Street wagons, those for Washwood Heath being, 'on the brake'. The terms 'on the engine or 'on the brake' were railwaymens' expressions describing where in the train the wagons were to be placed. If required we picked up additional wagons at Broom, though it was not a regular stop. We then went forward to Lawley Street, unless we had wagons to detach at Camp Hill.

Though the Beckford was a particular favourite of mine, it is perhaps not that typical of the working of a through freight train, if there is such a thing, so perhaps it would be instructive to examine another example of this type of train. The 5.30am, Mondays excepted, through freight from Peterborough to Birmingham Lawley Street provides a good example of a train that was remarshalled more than once during its journey. The train departed with traffic for Leicester, Nuneaton, Water Orton and Washwood Heath. At Saxby more wagons were attached. At Leicester all the traffic for that city was detached and other wagons were attached but before leaving the train was marshalled into station order. At Nuneaton the train was detached and, to quote the marshalling book it would, 'load forward Water Orton, exchange, Washwood Heath front fan.' This meant that some wagons would be left at Nuneaton and the train would depart with traffic for Water Orton, which would be detached and then attached to trains leaving Water Orton for other destinations. The train from

Peterborough then went to the front fan of sidings at Washwood Heath Down Sidings, part of a very large marshalling yard between Water Orton and Lawley Street. The wagons for Lawley Street remained with the engine but the rest of the train was detached. Then other wagons for Lawley Street were added to the train at Washwood Heath before the final part of the journey was undertaken. This is a particularly good example of how complex the working of through freight trains could be. I hope this might encourage modellers to increase the interest in the working of goods traffic on their layouts, by adding and subtracting wagons from their trains rather than just running the same block of wagons around all the time.

To see how this great interlocking system worked, let us now trace the route of a shipment from a station in north London which is to be consigned to Redditch in Worcestershire. The manufacturers would contact the railway carriers and ask for the goods to be collected from the factory. The railway vehicle, either horse drawn or a motor lorry, depending upon the date, would take the consignment to a goods station, in this case let us say St Pancras goods station, where the consignment would be loaded into a covered or open goods wagon. Depending upon the nature of the goods, if it was in an open wagon it might be sheeted over. We will assume that the consignment is an economic wagon load, say four tons in weight.

The wagon will form part of an express goods train that will travel to Birmingham Lawley Street goods station, where the London to Birmingham Midland Division trains were terminated. Our wagon would then be tripped to Washwood Heath sidings. From there it will form part of a train to Redditch. The Washwood Heath to Redditch service will be a through freight train but the Lawley Street to Washwood Heath train will be a local trip

working. At Redditch the consignment will be unloaded and a railway road vehicle will deliver the goods to their final destination. This service was known as, 'S to S', station to station. This is a typical example of how goods were efficiently conveyed carried across the kingdom in the days when the railways were the principal means of transporting goods and minerals throughout the country. This type of business is now unfortunately almost exclusively carried on the roads.

There was no such thing as a typical local trip working as they were extremely varied. One such duty could involve shunting every station goods yard over a 20 to 40 mile length of line. The men could work out and back or exchange with a crew working in the opposite direction at a half way point. It could even mean that the crew had to lodge away from home overnight, returning with a balancing working the following day. Such a trip working would detach loaded wagons at stations along the way, collect or detach empties and pick up loads for onward despatch.

Other trip workings were simple out and back trains from a marshalling yard to a single destination. For example a train of empty coal wagons would be taken from the yard to a colliery, where a rake of loaded wagons would be picked up to bring back to the marshalling yard. The delivery of a complete train load for a major industrial user could make up part of a trip working, with local goods pick ups occupying the return leg. Trip workings were as varied as the traffic in the area and offer endless permutations for the modeller.

At first sight the conveyance of mineral traffic is less complicated but this is not entirely true. Coal was loaded at the colliery into dedicated wagons, in the pre-BR era, many of these would have been privately owned by either the colliery, a coal merchant or a coal factor. The loaded coal wagons were taken away on a regular basis and while there could be through workings from the colliery to the end user, these were few in number during the period under review. It would be more usual for the coal wagons to go to a marshalling yard or sorting sidings were the traffic could be sorted before being sent in the general direction of its final destination. If this sounds rather vague, it is deliberate, for it is time to introduce the word 'rough' in its railway context. Rough was a railway expression used to describe a train of wagons that were not marshalled in station order. An example would be wagons loaded at

Kingsbury colliery in Warwickshire for Swindon and Taunton, both on the Great Western Railway.

We will assume that the coal is in local merchants' wagons and they have been correctly labelled at the colliery. There were several local trip workings daily that served the Kingsbury colliery branch. The loaded coal wagons would be tripped to Washwood Heath where they would be marshalled. The Swindon wagons would travel in a mineral train to Cheltenham. This would be a through working conveying traffic for Cheltenham and the area around it, together with any traffic for destinations on the former Midland & South Western Junction line which ran south from Cheltenham and was absorbed by the GWR in 1923. Our wagon of coal for Swindon would

be exchanged at Cheltenham and then it would be worked forward by the GWR, probably over the former M&SWR route to Swindon Town.

The route of the wagon of coal for Taunton could vary. Washwood Heath might send it on a coal train to Gloucester, or to Westerleigh yard in Bristol, as 'rough wests'. At Westerleigh it would be shunted into station order before forming part of a train to be sent to the GWR. There were no through workings from either Gloucester or Westerleigh to Taunton so the wagon of coal would be shunted into other trains at least once after it went onto the GWR. Whereas merchandise traffic was often conveyed long distances to its destination overnight, coal wagons could take several days to travel comparatively short distances.

Empties were returned the same way. In the days of the private owner wagon they were clearly marked with the name of the colliery where they were to be loaded. Their return journey would often be a slow one, from marshalling yard to marshalling yard. All coal wagons were pooled at the outbreak of the Second

World War. This common user policy led to an immense reduction in amount of shunting required now that it was no longer necessary to return a wagon to a particular colliery. Some care was still needed. For example there was no point in sending side door only coal wagons to a colliery to be loaded with coal for a customer who required it to be tipped and who thus needed to have the coal sent in wagons with an end door. Generally speaking however, post 1939 this area of railway operation was more straightforward.

Coal traffic was often worked by local trips from marshalling yards to industrial users in block trains, but coal for the domestic market went by stopping or through freight trains for the final part of the journey. Therefore on a model railway, a few loaded or empty coal wagons can be part of a train. In fact it would not be incorrect if a train had both loaded and empty coal wagons, the empties having been collected before the train arrived at the station where the loaded wagons were to be detached. Freight traffic offers endless opportunities for creative modelling.

Right: This view of a typical South Wales coal train is of interest in that the locomotive appears to be carrying what we would recognise as an express passenger headlamp code though this is really telling us that over the years the headlamp codes did vary. The locomotive is Rhonda & Swansea Bay 0-6-2T No 26, photographed at Court Sart station in 1919. The 0-6-2T wheel arrangement was popular in South Wales, where tank engines were preferred for working all sorts of traffic. All the wagons in this train are privately owned and uniform in size. Ken Nunn/LCGB

Below: This train, hauled by a Horwich Mogul No 2823, is running under the mineral train headlamp code. In railway terms the leading vehicle, a cattle wagon, would be described as being, 'on the engine'. Behind this are a number of loaded mineral wagons, but further back there are a variety of goods vans and wagons. An important operating principle is illustrated here namely that loaded livestock vehicles were to be marshalled next to the engine and not elsewhere in a loose coupled train such as this.

Top: **Not all goods trains were lengthy. This picture, taken at Derby in 1926, shows what modellers generally describe as a pick up goods, but which the railway staff would usually refer to as a stopping freight train. This example is a local trip working, it carries an identification target board bearing the number 2 attached to the right lamp iron. Such boards were often carried by local trip workings to assist signalmen in identifying these trains in an area where several such working operated. Generally trip workings conveyed far more than the** two wagons seen here but such very short workings did appear from time to time.
W L Good

Above: **Taken near Haresfield on the Gloucester and Bristol line in 1936, this picture shows a LMS Class 4F No 4272 at the head of a through freight train, probably a working from Bristol to Gloucester. The composition of the train is of interest. Virtually every open goods wagon has been sheeted over to protect the load. Just think of the amount of work** which this created as there are rather more open wagons than covered goods vans on the train. This is a very typical view of the mixed freights of this period. The location, between Tuffley Junction and Standish Junction, is also of interest. here for a distance of just over four miles, GWR and LMS tracks ran alongside each other. The lines to the far left of the picture are those of the GWR.

Below: **By the 1930s the railway companies had growing fleets of modern mixed traffic locomotives which could be used on the most important express freight workings. In previous years, it was the usual practice to use express passenger engines to work these services. This picture shows** ex L&NWR 4-6-0 No 5676 at Carpenters Park in February 1928 working the 2.50pm. Camden to Glasgow goods. The train is comprised of 25 covered vans and a brake.

Bottom: **BR built thousands of steel bodied mineral wagons in the 1950s which largely** replaced older wooden bodied types on mineral trains. In May 1962, 8F No 48185 heads through Stapleford & Sandiacre station at the head of a mineral train, largely composed of 16 ton steel bodied mineral wagons.

MIXED TRAINS

In view of the large number of branch lines modelled today, I am surprised that so few operators take the opportunity these lines offer to include mixed trains within the operating sequence. Perhaps many contemporary modellers find it difficult to believe that they existed. They did, as the two photographs on this page show. In order to provide operational legitimacy for these trains, one need look no further than the General Appendix to the LMS 1937 Working Timetable from which the extracts below have been taken. The operating instructions for mixed trains on the other railway companies' lines were virtually identical to those of the LMS. The relevant section of the Working Timetable reads as follows;

1. 'Mixed' trains for the conveyance of freight and passengers, in which the freight wagons are not required to have continuous brakes, may be run, subject to the following conditions, namely:

(a) That the engine, tender and passenger vehicles of such 'mixed' trains shall be provided with continuous brakes worked from the engine.

(b) That the freight wagons shall be conveyed behind the passenger vehicles with the brake van, or brake vans, in the proportion of one brake van with a tare of 10 tons for every 10 wagons, or one brake van with a tare of 13 or more tons for every 15 wagons, or one brake van with a tare of 16 or more tons for every 20 wagons, or fractional parts of 10,15 or 20 wagons respectively.

(c) That the total number of vehicles of all descriptions of any such 'mixed' train shall not exceed 30, except in the case of a circus train, when the number shall not exceed 35.

(d) That all such trains shall stop at all stations, so as to avoid a longer run than 10 miles without stopping, but nothing in these regulations shall require a stop to be made between two stations should the distance between them exceed 10 miles. The distance over which a circus train may run without a stop may be increased to a maximum of 50 miles.

2. Upon lines where the maximum speed of trains is limited to 25 miles per hour, all trains may be 'mixed'.

Upon lines where no trains are booked to travel between stations at an average speed of more than 35 miles per hour, half of the total number of passenger trains may be 'mixed'. Authority to work a larger number of 'mixed' trains must be obtained from the Minister of Transport.

Upon lines where trains are booked to travel between stations at an average speed exceeding 35 miles per hour, the like authority must be obtained before any 'mixed' trains are run.

Circus trains may be run without such authority during the period from 31st March to 30th November in any year whether the maximum average speed of trains run on the section of line concerned is limited or not.

In no case must the speed of a circus train exceed 30 miles per hour.

3. Trains for the conveyance of horses, cattle or other stock, when vehicles are added for the conveyance of passengers, shall be subject to the same regulations and conditions as apply to 'mixed' trains, but drovers, grooms or other persons travelling in charge of stock shall not be deemed to be passengers.

A passenger vehicle provided for the special accommodation of persons travelling in charge of stock must, however, be marshalled next to the engine, and be provided with the continuous brake worked from the engine.

4. When, in addition to one goods brake van at the rear of a 'mixed' train, a passenger brake vehicle is included as part of the continuously braked stock, it will not be necessary for a guard to ride in the passenger brake vehicle. If the composition of the train necessitates a second (or third) goods brake van, a second (or third) guard will be necessary, unless communication between the vans is such as to enable to operate efficiently the hand brakes on the vans.

All trains booked to run as 'mixed' will be so shown in the Working Time Tables, and all the foregoing regulations will apply to such trains.

The expression circus train means a 'mixed' train in which livestock, traction engines, trailers, caravans, tenting and other equipment and circus employees belonging to a touring circus are exclusively being conveyed.

Left: **The two pictures of mixed trains seen here were both taken on the Dornoch branch in the north of Scotland. The upper picture was taken in LMS days at The Mound, where the branch met the Inverness to Thurso line. The other view is of a train shunting at Dornoch on 4th September 1952. As photographed, neither train conforms to the regulations set out above. No 15054 requires a goods brake van to make the train complete. In the lower picture No 55051 is shunting. The goods brake would not be the second vehicle in the formation if it was preparing for departure. Both locomotives are ex Highland Railway 0-4-4Ts. No 15054 was withdrawn in 1945 but as BR No 55051, the other engine survived until 1956.**

ENGINE SHEDS

Notwithstanding the number of books that have been published about engine sheds, and the fact that they were visited frequently by enthusiasts in the days before the end of steam, it is probably true to say that they are often incorrectly portrayed on many model railways. On many layouts engine sheds appear in locations where in reality a shed would not have been built on the prototype. Another common fault is that the layout of the depot does not represent prototype practice. In the days of steam it was possible to visit sheds, usually on a Sunday, as part of an organised group. On these occasions the sole objective for almost everyone, was to write down as many engine numbers as possible. Therefore it is not too surprising that even modellers who were able to visit sheds in the days of steam, did not really study what was going on. It could also be argued that a Sunday is not a typical working day, which makes the personal observations of older modellers unrepresentative of the day-to-day working practices at motive power depots. Therefore I will begin this section with a brief description of what happened at sheds day by day.

Steam locomotives were allocated to engine sheds on the basis of the work that was to be undertaken. At some major centres one large shed sufficed, at others two were necessary, usually one for passenger traffic, and the other for freight. The number of locomotives stationed there generally dictated the size of the shed, but this did not always apply. The opening of new lines in an area, which led to an increase in traffic, meant more locomotives. Some sheds thus became too small for the number of locomotives allocated there. In some cases the depot was rebuilt. As always with railway modelling the best advice is to study the prototype rather than copy other modellers.

The job of a shed was to prepare locomotives for duty and dispose of them when they had completed their duties. Drivers and firemen were rostered on a daily basis and although some were spare, with no booked work, cover for those who were sick or on holiday or there to be available to work any extra trains required, most crews had booked duties. The procedure at all sheds was the same. When a crew arrived to prepare a locomotive and to work a specific duty, they would book on, read the traffic notices and find the locomotive that had been allocated to them. While the driver oiled and examined the locomotive, the fireman would prepare the fire and ensure that he had all the required tools. He would also fill the sandboxes. The importance of sand at engine sheds is often overlooked by modellers. Most sheds had a sand oven though at smaller sheds which did not, dry sand was delivered with the stores and kept in sacks or

Below: **Engine sheds came in a variety of sizes, this example, the Great Western shed at Ross-on-Wye is typical of the smaller type of shed which is so beloved by modellers. This shed could keep two engines under cover. One of these, a 48XX 0-4-2T, can be seen inside the shed. The auto trailer, No 84, which this locomotive would have hauled in service, can be seen on the siding adjacent to the shed. At a shed of this size, no repairs other than those of a very minor nature would be carried out. The locomotives would go to a larger depot for boiler washouts and examinations.** W A Camwell

Bottom: **Shunting locomotives at major marshalling yards and goods stations were often on duty for a 24 hour period between leaving the engine shed and returning. After the introduction of the eight hour day for railwaymen, this meant that a three shift system was used. Where a locomotive was working at a distant yard, the first shift**

would prepare the engine and bring it to where it was to work. A second crew would relieve the first shift and a third set of men would eventually return the locomotive to the engine shed. Depending upon the circumstances, some servicing would be necessary during the long period the engine was away from its shed. At the very least the fire would need to be cleaned and perhaps extra coal would be required. Many depots had small servicing points where this could be done. This picture shows the arrangements at Sheffield Queens Road goods station. The essential requirements are here, a pit to enable the enginemen to go beneath the locomotive for inspection, oiling round and to rake out the ashpan. There is also a coal stage. A coal wagon would usually be stationed on the siding to the right of the picture. One other vital requirement is missing from the picture but was certain to have been located nearby, namely a water column.
R S Carpenter collection

dry bins. Locomotive sheds could be either roundhouses or straight sheds or sometimes a combination of both styles. In a roundhouse engines were stabled on roads radiating from a central turntable. Because the roundhouse takes up a lot of room, most modellers build straight sheds. At these depots on the full size railway it was usual to stable the engines turned correctly for their next duty. Getting to the turntable to turn a locomotive at a busy shed that was not a roundhouse could be time consuming.

Most engines would be prepared inside the shed and the inside roads generally had full-length inspection pits to enable the engine-man to go beneath his engine. At some places, locomotives were also prepared in the open so inspection pits were to be found outside the shed. Once the locomotive was ready to depart one of the final tasks was to top up the tanks with water. The locomotive head and tail lamps would be positioned and the fire irons, usually a clinker shovel, straight dart and rake would be safely stowed.

The sequence for disposal began when the engine came back onto the shed at the end of its duties. Water would be taken if it was low but otherwise filling the tank would wait until the locomotive departed for its next turn of duty. If the locomotive was to remain in steam there would need to be enough water left in the tank to keep it simmering until it was next required. The arrangements for disposal, which could vary from shed to shed, began by taking on coal. Then the fire was cleaned and the ashpan was raked out over a pit. Finally the smokebox was cleaned out. Not all locomotives were placed inside the shed, on many occasions they would have to stand outside in the shed yard.

When the engine was parked, what happened next would depend on whether it was left in steam or left dead, this term meaning that the fire had been totally removed. Engines which remained in steam were looked after by a steam raiser and it was during the time the engine was on shed that the engine cleaners would be able to do their work. Major repairs would usually be undertaken when engines were dead. The work undertaken at the depots depended upon circumstances and the size of the shed. Modellers often leave a wheel set in the yard at their shed, though this was a most unlikely event in reality.

Over the years some sheds were enlarged piecemeal but despite this at times they could become very congested leading to long delays in disposing of locomotives. During the 1930s, in an attempt to improve matters, some new sheds were built. The shed at Didcot, today famous as the base of the Great Western Society, being an example. Other improvements were introduced at some sheds such as mechanical coaling stages and hoppers for ash removal. The track layout was also remodelled in some cases.

On a model there should be movement as the locomotives go through the various activi-ties described above, but judging by personal observation at exhibitions, I find that most modellers just run their engines onto the shed and leave them on display until they are required again. On Dewsbury there was an operator who controlled the engine shed only. He would move engines that came onto shed through the sequence of coaling and ash pit work before running on to the turntable to turn. Perhaps surprisingly, some tank engines also needed to be turned. For example a shunt-ing engine would run either chimney or bunker first depending upon two factors. The first was whether it was driven from either the left or the right hand side of engine. This was important in that it determined on which side of the footplate the driver stood. The second factor was where the shunter was likely to be at the yard being worked. The driver would need to see the shunter so if it were necessary the engine would work bunker first to give him the best chance of seeing the shunter' hand sig-nals.

Some locomotives came onto a shed to take on coal and to clean the fire and then, stand out of the way, until they were required to leave the shed, their crew remaining with the locomotive all the time. Others would be placed inside the shed remaining there until they were required. On Dewsbury we did have some engines that came onto shed to turn, take water and then depart, but most went into the shed emerging later onto the outside pits where they stood for a while until, in our imag-ination, they were oiled and examined. It was the duty of the engine shed operator to have the engine standing at the shed exit signal ready to depart as soon as the main line sig-nalman could accept the locomotive. He would not be popular if the engine was late off shed.

As most modellers build smaller depots, per-haps a word about them would not be out of place. The depot which supplied the locomo-tives for branch lines would be at the terminus of the line or at the junction with the main line, that is if there was a shed there at all. Some branch lines had their motive power supplied from a main depot many miles away. When the engine shed was at the branch terminus it usu-ally would accommodate just the single loco-motive which was sufficient to work all the traffic on the branch, both passenger and freight. If there was just one locomotive the staff would probably be two drivers and fire-men, and a permanent night cleaner, who also acted as steam raiser and would in addition probably be responsible for coaling the loco-motive. Tank engines worked most branch lines but some saw tender locomotives. If there was no turntable at the terminus, tender first running occurred. As this happened on the prototype, it can also be done on a model.

Not all locomotive servicing was undertaken at engine sheds, other servicing points were used. For example, at many major stations there were one or two sidings where locomo-tives could be serviced. It was possible to clean the fire and smoke box without access to a pit though one was required to rake out the ash-pan. Coal was generally not available at these locations, though a turntable and a water col-umn would be found there. Similar servicing points could also be found at marshalling yards and goods stations adding to the already considerable opportunities for creative model-ling which engine sheds present.

All locomotives carried additional equip-ment, some of which was visible on the outside of the machine. What was carried varied over the years from company to company. During the nineteenth century, in particular on the smaller railways, re-railing jacks were to be seen attached to some locomotive's platforms. Locomotive lamps, fire irons, buckets, slaking pipes to water the coal to keep the dust down, and coal picks were common features on engines, as were storm sheets on many tender locomotives.

In addition to the equipment to be found on locomotives, there should also be tools and equipment around the shed. Features which can be a part of shed scenes include the stores van which delivered items such as brake blocks, fire bars and oil on a regular basis. Ash and clinker were carried away in open wagons which can be modelled. A careful study of pho-tographs will provide plenty of inspiration for creative modellers.

Opposite page, top: **When a locomotive came onto shed for disposal, a railway term that described the work that was undertaken prior to the engine being stabled in the engine shed, it was necessary to clean out the smokebox, clean or drop the fire and to rake out the ashpan. This May 1935 picture shows a LMS 'Jubilee' class 4-6-0 with a fireman cleaning out the smokebox. The ash will be shovelled into the pit and depending upon the facilities available, either be moved via an ashplant, (see below), or will be shovelled into into an empty wagon. This view was taken at Edge Hill shed in Liverpool. W Potter**

Opposite page, centre left: **LMS shed modernisation schemes saw the introduction of labour saving devices at many locomotive sheds. This picture shows the ash plant at Crewe South locomotive depot, with a tub of smokebox ash or clinker being tipped into an open wagon.**

Opposite page, centre right: **Whilst some sheds had mechanical coaling plants, many more remained labour intensive. This view shows the Southern Railway shed at Ashford in July 1946, with Class F1 4-4-0 No 1078 standing on the coaling stage road. Here coal from the wagons above was loaded onto tubs which were tipped by hand into the tenders below.**

Right: **Engine pits were used for inspection, preparation and disposal purposes. Inspection and preparation pits could be either inside or outside of the shed, disposal pits were always in the open. Generally they were equipped with a hosepipe that was used to damp down the ashpan prior to raking out. Note the recess on the left-hand side of the pit where the hosepipe was placed in this disposal pit at Tebay, photographed in 1964.**

Top left: **The great majority of engine sheds in Great Britain were straight sheds. Some had through roads, others were dead ended as seen here at Tunbridge Wells West in this 1907 picture. A feature of the inside of sheds was an arrangement to take away the smoke from locomotives in steam. Inspection pits often ran the full length of the shed roads with the floor of the pit sloping to allow water to drain away. The floor was usually built up to railhead level. The clean and tidy shed interior contrasts favourably with the conditions which were evident during the final years of steam.**

Top right: **This view of Redditch engine shed, photographed around 1952 some years after it was rebuilt with a new roof, is included as this shed is of a size that will appeal to many modellers of branch lines. Apart for the coaling stage, which was similar to that shown on page 81, everything else can be seen. To the left there is the staff cabin and stores while in the centre the water crane and fire brazier are prominent. Note the steps leading down into the inspection pit and the fire irons, some on the ground, others in the rack.**

Above: **The Great Western shed at Pontrilas is an example of a small shed serving a branch line, which was located at the branch's junction with the main line and not at the terminus. Pontrilas station was located between Hereford and Abergavenny and was the junction for the branch which ran up the Golden Valley to Hay-on-Wye. There is a wealth of detail in this picture which would look really good on a model.**

Right: **In these two pictures we are back in the territory where we have to check very carefully just to make sure that what we are looking at is really a model. They show just how good a recreation of the steam era can be achieved in model form. The upper view is a good example of a small branch line engine shed for one locomotive. At these locations coaling was often done from a wagon on an adjacent track. The provision of a coaling stage with a roof, as is modelled here, was something of a luxury.**

Below: **Both these are models have been executed in 7mm/Gauge 0. The model below is of a typical small GWR coaling stage with a large water tank above. The locomotive coal wagons were propelled up the coal road into the covered area where the coal was unloaded into skips. These in turn were pushed onto the ramps that enabled the coal to be tipped into the locomotive's tender or bunker.** Both, Tony Wright

SHUNTING

Shunting is a term that can be applied to a variety of movements on a railway. It is used to describe the movement of a complete train from one line to another or the positioning of engines at a locomotive shed. However, it is most commonly associated with the sorting of vehicles at marshalling yards.

In order to understand why shunting was necessary we must return to the subject of traffic. In a railway sense the word traffic has many meanings. Today when we travel by train, we are called customers by the modern railway companies, though we used to be described as passengers. To the railway companies then, we were passenger traffic and while we did not require shunting, the vehicles in which we travelled sometimes did. Parcels were also a traffic category and this was conveyed in either the passenger brake van or in purpose built vehicles that were attached or detached from trains along the way. This attaching and detaching is a form of shunting. As we have seen earlier (see pages 78 and 79) a wagon full of coal would probably be shunted or remarshalled several times before it reached its destination. The wagon load goods traffic common in the age of steam led to lots of shunting and shunting cost money. The railway companies did not engage in this unless it was absolutely necessary.

There were many types of shunting, flat, loose, gravitational (hump), fly or towrope. Although it was usually done with locomotives, horses, capstans and men were also used. If men were required to push wagons into position where other means were not safe or practical, pinch bars were often used to move the wagon's wheels. Horses were used for shunting until well into the British Railways period though quite how they and men with pinch bars can be turned into working models I do not know!

The technique known as fly shunting involved an engine pushing wagons ahead of it and then braking. The wagons could then be diverted into a different siding to the engine. It was prohibited except at places where there were no other reasonably practicable means of performing the work. Many modellers talk about fly shunting, when they actually mean loose shunting. Tow roping was a similarly dangerous practice that was only carried out where no other means were possible. This involved a locomotive on one track shunting wagons on another by means of a tow rope. These activities are difficult to recreate on a model railway.

One feature which can be modelled is the capstan which was used to shunt wagons in some locations, usually in goods sheds, warehouses and coal drops. On the real railway wagons were hauled by capstans to be positioned. Whilst this action cannot be modelled, the capstans themselves can be positioned in

suitable places in goods yards. and can be modelled.

This leaves flat or loose shunting, two names that describe the same thing, and hump or gravitational shunting, again two names for a similar method of shunting. Dealing with the latter first, one well known example of where this occurred was at the yard at Edge Hill in Liverpool. Here the whole yard was on a falling gradient. Most gravitational shunting was done over an artificial hump. Wagons were pushed to the top of the hump and as they rolled down the other side by gravity, they could be diverted into a number of sidings, their progress being slowed by retarders on the track or by shunters armed with brake sticks. It is not really practical to try to model this arrangement in anything other than a very large scale. With the small scales the lack of weight means that the stock may not roll far enough and if it did then stopping the wagon in the right place is difficult.

By far the largest amount of shunting carried out on the British railway system could be described as flat or loose shunting. Marshalling yards were designed to receive incoming trains, break them up and reassemble the wagons into new trains to be worked forward. A train would arrive on the reception or arrival line. The wagons would then be moved, by an engine to a headshunt, shunting line or shunting neck, three names for the same thing. The usual arrangement was for the shunting engine to draw the wagons back along the shunting line and for the head shunter to look at the wagon labels in order to decide where to make the cuts, in other words, where to divide up the train. When this was done the shunter would uncouple the first cut and call the driver forward. The driver would accelerate his engine to get the wagons rolling and then slam on the brakes. Whilst the rest of the train would stop, the uncoupled wagons would roll forward. Other shunters would, in response to the Head Shunter's shout or signal, have already set the road, so that the wagons would go into the correct siding. Where necessary, shunters would chase after the wagons in order to slow them down if they were going too quickly. This was accomplished by dropping the hand brakes and if required, pinning down the hand brake lever with a brake stick. The movement of the shunting engine was, forward stop, forward stop, forward stop. Shunting on model railways is, forward, stop, back, stop, forward, stop, and so on. It can be very difficult to reproduce on a model what used to happen on the full size railway, Fortunately not many modellers try to reproduce flat marshalling yards.

Every so often the shunter would call the shunting engine forward in order to close up the wagons on the siding. This was because wagons would bunch up at the end of the siding where the shunting was taking place and would soon foul other roads, hence the need to push them further along the siding in order to leave room for more wagons. For those

wondering why wagons did not run out of the other end of the siding, the answer is that the first two or three wagons had their brakes pinned down hard to prevent this happening. When the guard, prior to departure was examining the train, he would walk round, lift the brakes, couple all the wagons together and make sure they were all ready to travel. This was usually done before the train engine backed on, although if there was a gap and the wagons required closing up, this could not be done until the train engine arrived. Illustrations of typical types of wagon couplings will be found on page 88.

As goods stations are more common on model railways than large marshalling yards, the shunting techniques used there during the steam era will be of more interest to the modellers. Goods stations varied enormously in size. At one extreme there was the small station that saw just one stopping freight train per day, which was shunted by the goods guard assisted by the station porter. Depending upon circumstances the train could be left on the main line and the necessary wagons detached and attached, or the train could be put inside the yard in order to clear the main line.

When the train started its journey it would have been marshalled in station order but if there were a number of stops where wagons were attached and detached the wagons would get somewhat mixed up. Nevertheless the guard would know what he was doing and the work would be carried out using the railway principle of, the least number of moves to complete the work. At small goods stations there was less opportunity to work on the forward, stop, forward principle, so the modeller's method of shunting does not look too out of place. As well as picking up loaded wagons, the engine would place any wagons it had brought that were to be loaded or unloaded, in the appropriate part of the yard, before it departed.

At the other extreme there were the large urban goods stations where the bulk of the railways freight traffic both originated and terminated. Some depots had their own marshalling yards while others only received traffic that had arrived elsewhere and been shunted into final destination order before being tripped to the goods depot. Shunting at these depots was by horse, capstan or with wagons being moved from one line to another by a wagon turntable. Tractors were not unknown and finally there were shunting engines. The train engine often undertook a large amount of shunting especially when making up its train prior to departure from these major depots. This supplemented the work of the depot's own shunting engines.

There were few rules about the make up of trains and most of these could be broken! Most modellers would tell you that a goods train on the main line must have a brakevan at the rear but there were locations where this rule did not apply. I will conclude this section about freight trains with a few notes about the composition of trains. Some years ago, my good friend Don Rowland published some research on the types of goods wagons in service in the late 1930s. This work is still very relevant for modellers who are deciding what types of stock they should have on their layouts.

He analysed the wagon stock of the LMS in 1938 showing that out of a total revenue earning fleet of 285,611 vehicles, 147,811 were open goods wagons and 51,220 were covered goods vans. The company's had 62,509 mineral wagons, 7,272 cattle wagons, 3,450 special wagons and 7,732 rail and timber trucks. There were 5,617 brake vans weighing over 15 tons with just 202 at less than 15 tons. Service vehicles came to 14,488. The total company stock was 300,099. The LMS owned more wagons than the other three main line companies but this total was dwarfed by the number of privately owned wagons. These came to 605,009 vehicles, all except 21,310 of these being mineral wagons. The wagons owned by the other companies were; LNER 258,236, GWR 82,453 and SR 33,709, with 3,580 on minor lines. The LMS owned 43% of the wagon stock, the LNER 39%, the GWR 12.4% and the SR 5.1 %, with the minor lines contributing only 0.5%.

The underlying message to modellers, confirmed by observation of most model railways, is that there are too many vans and not enough open goods wagons. Furthermore claims for compensation for damaged goods would be high judging by the number of loads that ought to be sheeted over, but are not!

Top: **Despite evidence to the contrary in this WR scene where 57XX pannier tanks are shunting goods stock, open wagons far outnumbered vans in the steam era.** D F Tee

Centre: **Hump shunting was usually undertaken at large yards, though not always, as this picture taken at Nuneaton shows. Ex-LNWR 0-8-0 No 49441 is about to push three 16 ton mineral wagons over the hump. Two shunters are standing by the wagon next to the locomotive, the small hut to the left was designed to give some protection to the shunters during bad weather conditions.**

Bottom: **This picture, taken at Heaton Norris, Stockport in 1964, when capstans and wagon turntables were still in use, shows how long lived were goods handling practices developed in the Victorian era. The wagon turntables enabled a wagon to be moved from one line to another. They could be turned through 90 degrees from the sidings to be moved into the warehouse. There are four turntables, side by side, connecting the sidings. Although the rope that was used can be seen, only two capstans are visible, one between the two left hand tracks, with the man in a white shirt is leaning against the other.**

Left: **The work of the shunter on the steam railway was arduous and would today be considered very hazardous. In this view a shunter is wielding his traditional shunter's pole which was used to couple or uncouple wagons with two or three link couplings. Here the wagons are 'buffered up', meaning that they are being compressed by an out of sight locomotive. The links of the coupling have thus been slackened and can be seen below the level of the buffers. In this position it is easy for the shunter to uncouple the wagons. When a train consisting of wagons with this type of coupling starts off, the couplings between each wagon will be stretched down the length of the train as it gets underway. Too much of a jerk from the locomotive could cause a coupling to break. On wagons like these the only type of brake provided was the hand brake. In this scene, the hand brake of the covered goods van to the right of the man has been pinned down, it will have to be lifted before the wagon is moved.** NRM Derby Collection DY13328

Centre: **This illustrates the Instanter coupling. These could be set, in either the long or short positions. When coupled in the long position it was possible to flick them into the short position with a shunting pole. It was quicker than tightening screw couplings although the instanter coupling was somewhat heavier than a normal three link coupling.**

Bottom: **This is a close up of the connections between two braked or fitted goods wagons. The one on the left is certainly braked as evidenced by the brake shoe on the wheel beside the shunter's pole. The procedure for uncoupling such stock was similar to that discussed earlier in relation to passenger stock. Once the wagons had come to rest, first off was the vacuum brake hose or in railway parlance, the 'bag'. This applied the brakes and meant that it was safe to go under and deal with the coupling, in this case a screw coupling. The piece of metal hanging down with the ball at the end, was the handle for tightening or loosening the coupling. Here, the vehicles are buffered up but the screw coupling is still slack. The guard or shunter in the picture will need to tighten it up before departure. The chalk marks made by shunters on the end of the left hand wagon were often seen and if replicated, would add a nice touch of realism to a model.**

LAMPS & SIGNS

There are some items that can add to the overall realism that modellers wish to achieve, which are sometimes overlooked. An example is the use of signs and notices. These were frequent sights on the real railway, they are noticeably less common on model railways.

Another instance is the tail lamp. On the real thing, the absence of a tail lamp was a serious matter. If the tail lamp could not be seen by the signalman as a train passed his box, he had to act as if it had divided in the section, with some vehicles left behind to block the line. He had to stop the train and have it examined. Locomotive headlamps, discs or indicators, as prescribed by the railway companies were also vital as they identified the class of train and sometimes its destination. The rules that covered this aspect of full size railway work are unfortunately ignored by most modellers.

The rules in relation to lamps on freight trains were quite complex. To give a flavour of these, the tail lamp codes below are abstracted from the 1937 Appendix to the LMS Working Timetable, but they also applied to all British railway companies.

Mixed trains with a goods train guard's brake at the rear had to have side lights as well as a tail lamp. The positioning of the lamps varied according to the nature of the road being followed. On main lines where there are only two lines and on single lines, one red tail light and two red side lights were required. On routes where there were three or four running lines, if the train was travelling on the fast line one red tail light and two red side lights had to be carried whereas on slow, goods or loop lines the code was one red side light on the side of the van furthest away from the fast line, one white side light on the side of the van nearest the fast line and one red tail light. Finally, on goods or loop lines adjoining four main lines, one red tail light only was required and side lamps had to be removed when the train has passed into the loop.

Apart from some coaches equipped with buckeyes, either loose or screw couplings were used in Britain. Loose wagon couplings had at one time comprised five links though three was the usual arrangement during the twentieth century. The majority of wagon couplings were similar in size but the GWR introduced the Instanter coupling. This coupling could be used in either the long or short positions. In the long position this was not really any different from a three-link loose coupling but when in the short position it reduced the distance between the buffer faces and thus the coupling slack in the train. These could be considered an economy version of the screw coupling and they were used on vehicles that would benefit from a reduction of slack, such as cattle wagons or merchandise vehicles running in express goods trains. They were not fitted to locomotives.

The majority of locomotives were equipped with screw couplings. Those that were not were usually shunting or mineral engines not fitted with the automatic vacuum brake. One reason for not using screw couplings was expense but a better reason, was that it was easier to swing a three-link coupling with a shunters pole than it was to swing a screw coupling. It took longer to couple or uncouple two vehicles fitted with screw couplings.

If stock was fitted with continuous brakes, the sequence for uncoupling was always based on the principle that the first thing off and the last thing on, was the vacuum brake or Westinghouse air brake pipe. This was a basic safety provision, if the brake pipe was disconnected, the train could not move. Steam heating and electrical connections, on passenger stock would follow, finally the vehicles would be uncoupled. When vehicles were being coupled the order was reversed, the brake pipes being the last thing to be connected. When a screw coupling was involved, the fireman or shunter would have to take the time to turn the screw a few times before he could lift the link off the coupling hook. This took a minute or so to do. Therefore, modellers who wish to produce an authentic look to their operations should ensure that there is a definite pause in the proceedings when uncoupling is taking place. Often, a train would pull up with the coupling so taught that it was impossible to loosen the couplings. Here the shunter would have to ask the driver to set back a shade to loosen the couplings. This also took time. A locomotive setting back a fraction to loosen the couplings is something which one never sees happening on a model railway.

Above left: **In this picture, taken at the ex-LNWR station at Holywell in North Wales, three different signs can be seen. The gradient board, the short white angled post in the centre of the three, was commonplace, although the design varied slightly between the different companies. To the right of this, the white board carries the message, 'Goods trains to stop to pin down brakes'. Boards with this message for train crews were common at the top of inclines across Britain, though again the style of board varied from company to company. The severity of the grade here can be seen in the picture. The third sign warns of the trap points on the right hand track, which can also be seen.** J Moss

Above right: **Jersey Marine was a halt on the Rhondda & Swansea Bay Railway near Swansea. The line became part of the GWR in 1923. In this picture, taken in August 1949, original R&SB signs are still in place. This is not unusual as many such signs, especially those made of cast iron, were very long lived. One different thing about this crossing is the warning bell, seen on the pole in the centre, and the sign drawing attention to it. The notice informed users that the ringing of the bell indicated that a train was approaching.**

Top left: **At stations where passengers might have to change trains, it was usual to ensure that the information they would need was clearly displayed. Hope Exchange was in Flintshire, where the former Great Central line which ran roughly north to south from Wrexham to Birkenhead, crossed the L&NWR line running east to west from Chester towards Denbigh. This 1947 picture shows ex-GCR 4-4-2T No 7436 at the head of a passenger train at the GCR line station. Though this is correctly described as an LNER line on the sign, the pre-grouping ownership is still applied to the other line. W A Camwell**

Centre left: **This delightfully ambiguous sign was to be found by a bridge on the West London Extension Railway. It is difficult to see the point of as vague a warning as this.**

WEST LONDON EXTENSION RAILWAY
TO DRIVERS & OWNERS OF LOCOMOTIVES OR OTHER PERSONS IN CHARGE OF THE SAME IN PURSUANCE OF THE LOCOMOTIVE ACT OF 1898 NOTICE IS HEREBY GIVEN THAT THIS BRIDGE IS INSUFFICIENT TO CARRY ANY WEIGHT BEYOND THE ORDINARY TRAFFIC OF THE DISTRICT AND THE OWNER DRIVER OR OTHER PERSON HAVING CHARGE OF ANY LOCOMOTIVE IS HEREBY WARNED NOT TO ATTEMPT TO DRIVE OVER THIS BRIDGE WITHOUT HAVING PREVIOUSLY OBTAINED THE CONSENT OF THE WEST LONDON EXTENSION RAILWAY COMPANY BY ORDER

Below: **This sign, unusually positioned on a high pole and with a lamp to enable it to be seen at night, suggesting that its message was of some importance, warned that, 'engines must not pass this board unless authorised by the shunter or the person in charge of the train', It was photographed in April 1952 at the Ilkeston terminus of this former Great Northern Railway branch in Derbyshire. An ulterior motive for including this picture is that it offers an alternative track layout for a branch terminus. The two platform lines came together beyond the road bridge. A locomotive could leave its coaches on one platform line and use the other platform line to run round its train. This layout would make a change from the normal single platform face at a terminus station that many modellers use.**

Right: Trains were classified in a number of ways. They were described in the working timetables and each class of train had a distinctive bell code which was relayed between signal boxes. Another distinguishing feature was the headlamp code carried on the locomotive. All these features were subject to change over the years and also varied from company to company. Probably the most confusing and complex codes were those that gave route indication as well as the class of train. This view of LB&SCR Class B4 4-4-0 No 52 at London's Victoria station shows the array of locomotive headlamps and discs which that company used to provide its signalmen with the information they required about the train's identity and destination.

Above: Although there were some exceptions, the Somerset & Dorset Joint Railway being one, after 1903 most British railway companies used the Railway Clearing House standard headlamp codes. Prior to that date the variety to be seen was considerable. This pre 1903 picture shows one of the earlier non-standard headlamp codes as used on a Midland Railway train. Note the two lamp irons on the centre line of the engine, one on the top of the smokebox, the other on the smokebox door. There is no centre lamp iron, but, when facing the engine, there is one on the left hand side and two on the right, one with a lamp in place. The headlamp code for an express train on some companies prior to 1903 was two headlamps, placed in the positions shown here. NRM Adams Collection G559

Right: On lines with heavy traffic or where the locomotives of more than one company could be found, it was often considered necessary to provide railwaymen, in particular signalmen, with more information. One way this could be done was to fit identification headboards to the engines. This picture of MR 0-6-4T No 2004 was taken when the engine was working on the London, Tilbury & Southend section of the Midland Railway. The Upminster headboard is carried on additional bracket holders that have been fitted to the front of the locomotive. The arrangement and positioning of these brackets varied between companies. K Leech

TRAIN MOVEMENT

Although previously I had driven locomotives in the shed yard at Saltley and on occasion along a goods line when running light engine, the first time I drove a train on a main line was in May 1951. I will never forget the experience of that beautiful sunny day at Bromsgrove when we walked towards the Worcester to Washwood Heath Class H through freight train, headed by No 43284. We were to relieve the engine crew and work the train forward to Washwood Heath Up sidings. With a few yards to walk before we climbed onto the engine, my driver asked me if I knew the road to Washwood Heath. I replied that I did. He responded by asking, 'all the signals?' to which I answered, 'Yes'. 'You can drive', was all that he said. For the rest of my time with Driver Arthur Thorpe, I was allowed to drive on a regular basis on some of the least important jobs that we had in the Little Bristol link.

During the age of steam it took many years before a young man was passed for driving. Beginning as an engine cleaner he was first, passed for firing and then, after anything up to 20 or more years 'on the shovel', he became a passed fireman, that is a fireman passed for driving who was able to take charge of trains. Finally he was registered as an engine driver. Today, if advertisements are to be believed, you can become a driver on one of the preserved railways after a short weekend course. It all comes under the heading of, driver experience courses or something similar. In this section I have included some tips that I learnt many years ago driving the real thing, which just might be of some use to those driving the model version.

Most modellers drive cars and I suspect it is this experience that lies behind the fact that on many models of steam age layouts, the locomotives behave like motor cars rather than steam engines. I remember the advice given me, before I was allowed to drive a mineral train, 'Remember Bob, you've only got a brake on the engine and there could be several hundred tons ready to push you forward if you are not careful.'

I was taught that when you approached a stop signal with a loose-coupled train you must be aware of the gradients. If the line was falling slightly or even level, you should be prepared to stop short of the signal. If the couplings were stretched out the wagons could surge forward and push your engine forward. If you overran your stopping place on a goods line, with a set of trap points beyond the signal, you could find yourself derailed. Therefore the golden rule, when driving a loose-coupled goods or mineral train, was caution. You had to stop short of the signal. However that doesn't mean that you crawled around everywhere. Most modellers seem to drive up to signals in a manner not dissimilar to driving up to

traffic lights, a fast approach and then the brakes go on and they stop with the front of the car in line with the red light! Railway trains do not run like that.

Starting a loose coupled goods train was an equally problematic business. I have known a few drivers whose starting methods were designed to, 'wrap the guard around the brake wheel'. In other words the brake van was jerked into starting. This was not good driving. It was much better when starting to pick up every wagon and then, when you felt that you had the train moving, open the regulator to increase speed. To jerk the train so that the brake van goes from a stand to several miles per hour in one movement made the possibility of a broken coupling more likely. If your models have fixed automatic couplings, then it is not possible to reproduce this movement, which helps to explain why I prefer three link couplings. With three link couplings a careful driver can, pick up the train one wagon at a time. To drive in this manner is more realistic and in my case, it is the way Drivers Thorpe and Smith taught me how to do it.

You now have your train on the move and a number of factors; its length, weight and the class of train, govern the speed at which it travels. A mineral train, running along a goods line or a main line, with the distant signals in the clear position, would not crawl. Freight trains were classified in order of importance and the speed that they travelled over a section of line. The only difference that the size of locomotive made was the weight of train hauled. For example a Class 8F 2-8-0, hauling a mineral train would be expected to travel from A to B in the same time as a Class 2F 0-6-0, the only difference being that the Class 8 locomotive would be hauling a much heavier train.

To illustrate the relative speeds at which the various classes of freight trains ran, let us examine an extract from the LMS Western Division 1945 Point to Point Running Times for Freight Trains relating to the section of line between Rugby and Coventry. To simplify matters I have also used the 1950 British Railway codes, although the LMS ran empty wagon trains at Class F timings prior to this date.

'Classification and time in minutes with an allowance for starting', was the official sounding heading in the point to point timing book, but it could also be described as the comparative times various classes of trains took to cover the same distance. It is easy to calculate the different speeds at which these classes of trains ran. The relevance of this for modellers is that on a main line layout, with a reasonable length of run, trains should not all run at the same speed. Between Rugby and Coventry the times allowed were; Class C 15 minutes, Class D 17 minutes, Class E 23 minutes, Class F 24 minutes, Class H 28 minutes and Class J 28 minutes. No times were given for stopping (pick up) freight or light engines. These comparative times were, in railway terms, 'start to pass'. Expressed in crude terms, a fully fitted freight train would run at almost twice the speed of a

mineral train. The times for the Rugby to Coventry section were for a fairly level section of line. Gradients played a considerable part in determining section timings on the full size railway. Unless a model is of a specific stretch of heavily graded track such as that through Shap or Ais Gill, this is not a factor which need concern the modeller.

With fully fitted trains, with an automatic brake controlled from the engine operating on each vehicle in the train (these could include passenger, parcels and mail trains), the driver had the maximum braking power available. Nevertheless on the full size railways they did not drive in a similar manner to that seen on many model railways today. Although the acceleration of a powerful passenger tank engine hauling three coaches would be much better than a larger engine with a full load of coaches, the same principles apply. There would be a slow start and once the train was on the move a steady acceleration would take place until the train reached a speed that the driver judged would enable him to run the train to time.

Similar care should be exercised when stopping passenger trains. They do not approach a platform and suddenly stop. As they approached the station speed was steadily reduced and the final stop was gentle. The advent of modern electric motors makes it perfectly possible to reproduce in miniature the way steam locomotives ran on the full size railways.

Many model railways feature a station at the end of a branch line where the locomotive runs round its coaches before taking the train out of the station again. This is another area where more realism could be introduced into model railway driving practice. On most model railways the run round is at a slow constant speed, sometimes it is at very slow speed, almost as if the operator is trying to show onlookers how good are the slow running properties of the mechanism of the locomotive. However this is the wrong way to do it.

When the train has come to a stand at the terminus someone, the fireman or a shunter, would go between the engine and coaches and uncouple the vacuum pipes and then the screw coupling. The fireman would return to the engine and when signalled, this could be a hand signal or fixed signal, the engine would move slowly forward to be clear of the points that connected the platform line to the run round loop. There would be a pause while the points were changed and the signal is given to the driver to run round the train. When the driver was signalled away he would open the regulator and the engine would accelerate quickly. He would then close the regulator and the engine would coast, slowing down before the driver stopped it with the brake. Caution was required when the engine moved to couple up to the train, I remember being told that you should be able to close up to the buffers and to hold an egg between them without breaking it! This seemed a rather strange way of describing this move but the message was clear. The fireman would then couple the engine to the coaches and set the headlamp code. The guard was responsible for seeing that the tail lamp was moved to the other end of the train and everything was ready to depart. Light engine running should not always take place at a very slow speed, it is only when closing up to buffer stops, or rolling stock, or stopping at water cranes that a very slow speed is correct.

'Water is more important than coal', this was a statement made to me by more than one driver. This does not mean that you should have

Although I started work on the LMS and that is my preferred post grouping company, my major interest has always been in the railways of the Edwardian and Victorian eras. This is a period which should attract more modellers. Because there are fewer layouts around, those set in this era are generally well regarded and attract a lot more interest than yet another model of a GWR branch line, no matter how well it is executed. Another attraction of this period is that, generally speaking, trains were smaller. Therefore more can be made to fit in less space and lack of space is usually the modeller's major problem. Allow me to indulge myself therefore by having, as the last model illustration in the book, this view of a 4mm scale Midland Railway bogie single locomotive working on the Ambergate layout.

water cranes everywhere. Water was taken before the locomotive left the engine shed and then afterwards, as required. Water columns or cranes would be found at the platform ends of many principal stations but not all. They would be positioned on goods lines and in particular in marshalling yards where shunting engines were regularly employed. Junction stations, from where branch lines diverged, would often have them to enable the branch passenger engine to take water between trips along the branch. If the water was not available at the main line junction, then it would have to be provided at the branch terminus. During frosty weather a brazier, often referred to as a frost fire, would be found adjacent to the water crane. Modellers should remember to include stops for water in an extended operating sequence.

When approaching a signal which is at danger modellers must always remember that they are supposed to be controlling a train and not driving a motor car. Approach the signal slowly and if yours is an unfitted train, remember that you only have the engine brake to stop the train and that there are several hundred tons of unbraked goods train behind you. When the signal is pulled off remember that you cannot start by putting your foot on the accelerator. If the train is unfitted then there will have to be time for the fireman to unscrew the hand brake before the driver can start. When stopped, the the driver may have opened the cylinder cocks. These will have to be closed and the engine put into gear before it goes anywhere. Preparing to move a train takes time. It could take a minute or two after the signals have been pulled off before an unfitted train could be got under

way again. Acceleration should be steady while the driver picks up the train, and then, when he feels that the train is complete, more pronounced acceleration can take place. The difference between a model railway where the operator has a feel for what he is trying to reproduce and one where the approach is more one of, crash, bang wallop, is immense.

Perhaps I may conclude with a few words about driver training. The North London Group's Heckmondwike layout was built to show that P4 scale was a working proposition and with an emphasis on demonstrating realistically how a steam railway was operated. I was responsible for the operating sequence, which I would like to think improved each time the layout was exhibited. Ken York was the overall General Manager for the project.

By the time of the first exhibition I had moved to the Midlands had not been a regular visitor to the clubroom where the operators, both drivers and signalmen, had been trained and passed out. Just prior to the start of the exhibition although fully conversant with the sequence, I was told that I was not allowed to operate the layout. Ken made it very clear that he, the General Manager, had not passed me out for an active role, but I could help off stage. He was quite right, operating a complex layout in front of the public requires concentration and time spent practising to become familiar with the controls and features of the layout is time well spent. This leads me to suggest that maybe on the best layouts we will see operators tested and placed into links, which reflect their ability and knowledge, just as we were on the real thing all those years ago, or is this straying too far into the realms of fantasy?

Two items featured in the Glossary are illustrated here.

Above: **The auto train which served the Wallingford branch is seen at the terminus. All the Big Four used trains of this sort. No 1444 was one of a class of 0-4-2Ts built by the Great Western in the 1930s to replace** older engines on these types of workings. **The point of these trains was to avoid the need to uncouple the locomotive at termini. This often resulted in a scene like this where the coach remained coupled to the locomotive when it went on shed to take water.** R J Doran

Below: **In Britain engine sheds were generally either straight or roundhouses built around a turntable to give access to all roads. This pre-1923 view shows the arrangemnent of the half-roundhouse at Eastbourne on the London, Brighton & South Coast Railway.**

SOURCES & BIBLIOGRAPHY

There are many books which can be recommended to modellers who wish to build accurate models of the steam age railway. Whilst this bibliography and list of sources is by no means comprehensive, it should prove a useful starting point. This listing first and foremost sets down the sources which I have consulted in the preparation of this book, but it also offers some guidance to the sort of material which prospective modellers should be consulting when they are planning their layouts.In addition to the more comprehensive company histories and reference books, numerous books and articles have been published about various branch lines. Specialist booksellers are also usually happy to help in the selection and tracking down of reference material. Another approach which is worth considering is to join the Historic Model Railway Society or a society which specialises in the company in which one is interested.

Ashchurch to Barnt Green, the Evesham Route, Essery, Oxford Publishing Company, 2002.

Book of Instructions to Station Master, Signalmen and Other. Regulations for Train Signalling by the Absolute Block System, LMS, 1934.

Brewery Railways of Burton-On -Trent, Shepherd, Industrial Railway Society, 1996.

British Goods Wagons, Essery, Rowland and Steele, David & Charles, 1970.

British Railway Carriages of the Twentieth Century, Jenkinson, Patrick Stephens, 1988.

British Railway Modelling, A Century of Progress, Essery, Warner Group Publications, 2000.

British Railway Modelling, Classic Layouts, Essery, Warner Group Publications, 2001.

First Principles of Railway Signalling, Byles, Railway Gazette, 1918.

Great Western Way, Slinn, Historic Model Railway Society, 1978.

History and Development of Railway Signalling in the British Isles, Volume 1, Broad Survey, Friends of the National Railway Museum.

History and Development of Railway Signalling in the British Isles, Volume 2, The Telegraph, Friends of the National Railway Museum.

LMS Engine Sheds, Nos 1- 5, Hawkins and Reeve, Wild Swan Publications.

LMS Engine Sheds, Nos 6 & 7, Hawkins, Reeve and Stephenson, Irwell Press.

LMS Journal Preview Issue, Southwell Engineman, Wild Swan Publications, 2001.

LMS Rule Books, various editions and supplements.

LMS School of Transport, Salesmanship Manual, LMS, 1938.

LNWR Liveries, Davis, Dow, Millard, Talbot, Historic Model Railway Society, 1985.

London, Tilbury & Southend Railway and its Locomotives, Essery, Oxford Publishing Company, 2001.

North Eastern Record, Volumes 1-3, North Eastern Railway Association and Historic Model Railway Society, 1988-2001.

The Midland in the Edwardian Era, Essery, Model Railway Journal No 7, Wild Swan Publications.

Midland Record 3, 4, 7, 11, 15, Wild Swan Publications.

Midland Style, Dow, Historic Model Railway Society, 1975.

Passenger Train Formations 1923-1983, LMS-LM Region, Carter, Ian Allan, 1987.

Pictorial Record of LMS Signals, Warburton, Oxford Publishing Company, 1972.

Pictorial Record of LNWR Signalling, Foster, Oxford Publishing Company, 1982.

Railway Carriages in the British Isles, 1830- 1914, Hamilton Ellis, George Allen & Unwin, 1965.

Signalling in the Age of Steam, Vanns, Ian Allan, 1995.

The Victorian Railway, Simmons, Thames & Hudson, 1995.

GLOSSARY

This glossary of some of the terms used in the book is not intended to be comprehensive. I have become conscious over the years that the depth and extent of the railway knowledge of modellers varies considerably. In drawing up this glossary, I have assumed less rather than more railway knowledge as being the standard.

Absolute block system: a system of signalling designed to prevent more than one train from being in a section of track at any time.

Auto train: also known as a motor train or a push pull set, this consisted of a specially equipped locomotive and and a coach or coaches that could be driven from either the locomotive or end of the last carriage thus doing away with the need for the engine to run round its stock at termini.

Big Four: the term applied to the four companies, the GWR, LMS, LNER and SR, formed as a result of the government sponsored amalgamation in 1923.

Blind siding: a very short siding not used for traffic purposes, such as the continuation of a loop line beyond its junction with the main running line to a sand drag or a catch point.

Block instruments: see page 40.

Cassette board: a modelling solution to turning trains at the end of layouts. This is a board containing track onto which a train is run. The board can then be lifted and turned to enable the train to return to its starting place without remarshalling.

Cattle dock: a fenced platform level with the floors of wagons from which cattle and other livestock can be loaded.

Common user: from the time of the Great War, the railway companies began to allow certain wagons to go into a pool which could to be used by all participating companies. In the years of the Big Four, all freight wagons were assumed to be common user, unless marked otherwise.

Connections: a general term used to describe the points that connect various lines.

Continuous brake: a braking system running the length of the train, though not necessarily acting on every vehicle, which could be operated by the driver or the guard. In the steam era the vacuum and Westinghouse brakes were the most common types of continuous brake in use.

Cut: a term used by shunters for a batch of wagons separated from a train. Sometimes also called a raft.

Dead end siding: see blind siding.

Disc/disc signal: a small circular signal, normally, though not always, found at ground level. Also known as a ground signal or a dummy.

Electrical repeaters: instruments used in signal boxes to show the signalman the aspect of signals which he could not see from his box.

Finescale: wheel and track standards which are more accurate than the original course standards employed in the early years of model railways.

Fitted: a term applied to vehicles that were equipped with an automatic brake.

Fitted freights: express goods trains which were either formed entirely of braked vehicles or had a batch of such wagons next to the engine to increase its braking power.

Ground frame/stage: a small collection of point or signal levers, usually at ground level and out in the open, to control access to an adjacent siding or connection, some distance from the signal box which controlled the area. Sometimes the frame was released by a key at the end of a train staff in single line sections.

Ground signal: see disc/disc signal.

Holloware: manufactured metal items which could range from saucepans to dustbins.

Inside: a locomotive or a vehicle was deemed inside, when it had been placed out of the way of other trains, on a siding for instance.

Interlocking: points and signals that have been mechanically or electrically linked so that the signalman cannot set up a conflicting movement.

Junction: a place where two or more running lines diverged or came together.

Loading gauge: this defines the maximum height and width that vehicles cannot exceed, if they are to pass safely along a stretch of railway.

Locking bar: a long bar set below the railhead at a connection and arranged so that when the wheels of a vehicle or locomotive were in contract with it, the signalman could not pull any levers that would move the point and thus cause a derailment.

Loose coupled: unbraked vehicles coupled together by loose link couplings.

Marshalling: the process whereby a train is assembling in a particular order.

Modern era: this is generally applied to the post 1968 period following the elimination of steam traction on British Rail.

Motor train: see auto train.

Non revenue earning: work or stock that did not earn the railway company money, such as wagons or trains used to maintain the track.

NPCS: non passenger coaching (or carrying) stock. Rolling stock that did not carry passengers but which could run in passenger trains, such as horse boxes or parcel vans.

Out of gauge: all lines were subject to width and height restrictions. An out of gauge load or vehicle was one that exceeded the limits these imposed. See also, loading gauge.

Permissive block working: this was an exception, only permitted in certain defined and carefully controlled circumstances, to the principle which lay at the heart of the block signalling regulations, namely, that only one train was allowed to be in a section at a time.

Pinch bar: similar to a crowbar, this was applied to the wheels of wagons to manually shunt them over short distances.

Private owner wagons: rolling stock registered to run over railway companies' lines but not owned them. Sometimes also referred to as owners wagons.

Private sidings: lines serving industrial or other locations which were not owned by the railway companies.

Pre-grouping: the era of railway history up the to 31st December 1922 when the Big Four (see above), came into existence.

Raft: see cut.

Railway Clearing House: an organisation which recommended standards for railway companies, adjudicated in their disputes and apportioned shared revenues between them.

Rough: a term applied to a raft of wagons which were all mixed up and required shunting into order.

Roundhouse: a type of engine shed whose main feature was a central turntable, from which the roads used to stable the locomotives, radiated.

Safety points: a collective name for catch, throw off or trap points. Their function is explained in detail on pages 21-26.

Setting back: reversing an engine or train.

Sanitary tubes: ceramic products for dealing with human waste.

Scotch block: a heavy block of wood or iron that was used to prevent the unauthorised movement of vehicles.

Slaking pipe: provided water via the locomotive's injectors, which was used to keep the footplate clean and water the coal in the tender to keep down the dust.

Specially constructed wagons: wagons that were designed to carry specific loads and whose movements were controlled by the owning railway company.

Station limits: the area between the first home signal and the last starting signal in each direction.

Station order: this term was applied to the wagons of a goods train when they were marshalled in the order in which they would be delivered.

Straight dart: this was a metal tool carried on a locomotive which was used to remove clinker from the firebars in the engine's firebox.

Straight shed: an engine shed with roads that ran from the front to the rear of the building.

Switchblades: the moving ends of a point which determined the direction of travel.

Traffic pooling: an arrangement between two or more railway companies to combine the receipts on an agreed basis for traffic carried over a particular section of line.

Transhipping: goods traffic that is transferred from one wagon to another or from one form of transport to another during the course of its journey.

Trip: a short distance goods working.

Turnback trains: trains that terminate at a station and then return to their starting point.

Wrong line working: a movement travelling in the opposite direction to the normal for that stretch of track, perhaps because of a mishap or as a result of track repairs.

Yard: an alternate name for station limits or the area under the control of one signal box.